The

Condominium Buyer's

Guide:

What to Look for—and Look Out for—
in Resort, Residential and Commercial Condominiums

JAMES N. KARR

The

Condominium Buyer's

Guide:

What To Look for — and Look Out for —

in Resort, Residential and

Commercial Condominiums

FREDERICK FELL PUBLISHERS, INC.
New York, N.Y.

TO KRISTI

I would like to express my appreciation to Raymond E. King of the Boston law firm Peabody, Brown, Rowley and Storey, and George J. Fantini, Jr., Assist. V.P. of Boston's State Street Bank and Trust Co. for their continued assistance during the writing of this book. It is also important that Raymond E. King be acknowledged for the writing of the sample condominium legal documents that appear in Appendix C. And lastly, a special appreciation to Kristi Petersen Karr for her invaluable support in helping me to organize this book and carry it through to completion.

Library of Congress Card No. 72-97531

SBN-8119-0219-6

Published Simultaneously in Canada by

George J. McLeod, Limited, Toronto 2B, Ontario

MANUFACTURED IN THE UNITED STATES OF AMERICA

Table of Contents

8

Introduction

The condominium is no longer a concept! It is here to stay and offers a new, exciting way of life. Although many books and articles have been written about condominiums, very few have been written specifically to aid the prospective purchaser in analyzing the various types of condominium offerings. For this reason, the following guide has been designed to give the purchaser a step-by-step system for analyzing condominium offerings. Only by following such a system can the prospective purchaser expect to efficiently check all pertinent considerations. Such a system of analysis has been sorely needed, for the only previous literature available was the sales literature itself.

The overall objective of the guide is to help the condominium buyer reach a quicker and more confident purchase decision. Included in the guide are what areas to analyze, what questions to ask, what costs to check, and offerings to avoid.

The first section, UNDERSTANDING THE CONDOMINIUM CONCEPT, reviews the basic condominium concept and introduces the various types of condominiums being made available on the market today. The benefits and drawbacks of the different offerings are also considered.

The second section, CHOOSING THE RIGHT CONDOMINIUM, presents areas of analysis that the new purchaser should explore when analyzing a condominium offering. Included in the step by step system of analysis is how a simplified marketing study should be performed, what to look for in the legal documents, what design features to check, and how to analyze the management function. The last area to be analyzed, which is the most critical in any condominium purchase, is the financial area. For this reason, a substantial portion of the guide deals with the various financial obligations and benefits of condominium ownership. Many sample cost sheets of residential, resort, and commercial condominium offerings are presented for reference data.

Overall, it is recommended that in any offering analysis, one consult his tax consultant, lawyer, and banker. The purpose of this guide is not to eliminate such professional help, but to help the individual utilize it more efficiently through a better understanding of the offering plan.

UNDERSTANDING

THE CONDOMINIUM CONCEPT

BECAUSE CONDOMINIUM LIVING HAS BECOME A WAY OF LIFE, it is important that one truly understand the condominium concept and how it is being applied in residential, resort and commercial offerings. Such is the purpose of this section as it reviews the basic definition of the condominium and the responsibilities of condominium ownership. It then describes the various types of condominiums being made available on the marketplace today. The benefits of such condominium living are discussed for each of the condominium types and finally a comparison of the condominium and cooperative forms of ownership is made.

Upon completion of this section, UNDERSTANDING THE CONDOMINIUM CONCEPT, one should gain a better insight into whether condominium living is truly for him.

I. Definition of a Condominium

In just the past 10 years, the condominium concept of ownership has made significant progress in the United States in offering to the public an exciting new way of life. Apartment ownership, business office ownership, and resort ownership, all in multi-unit complexes, is now available in many sections of the country. Nevertheless, there continues to be much confusion as to what "condominium" really means, and how the condominium idea works.

The word "condominium," although relatively new to the United States, has been in existence as a legal term meaning "joint ownership" as far back as ancient Roman law. The concept has long been extensively utilized in Western Europe and in Puerto Rico. In 1961, legislation was enacted in the United States on a federal level which authorized the use of condominium ownership. This type of ownership allowed for *individual ownership of a single unit in a multi-unit building or complex of buildings.* Along with the ownership of the single unit, each owner would own an undivided share of the common areas and facilities of the building complex; i.e., land, foundation, central heating and plumbing systems, hallways and entranceways, roof, recreational facilities, etc. Since that federal authorization, individual states have enacted their own statutes to further define condominium ownership. (See State Statutes & Regulations—Appendix A)

16

II. Responsibilities of Condominium Ownership

The responsibilities of ownership under the condominium concept are very similar to the ownership responsibilities of a single family home. The condominium unit may be mortgaged in the same manner as the single family home, and because it is considered an individual parcel of real estate, it is assessed for the collection of real estate taxes as is a single family home. Condominium ownership also requires that a budgeted monthly maintenance fee be paid to cover all costs of maintaining and managing the condominium property. An organization of condominium unit-owners, or administrators of the property, usually hire a professional management company to carry out the management function.

More detailed descriptions and analyses of the condominium owner's responsibilities will be covered in subsequent sections.

III. Types of Condominiums

The development of condominiums in the United States first started in the early 1960's in such states as Utah, California, Colorado, Florida, and New York. At the present time, condominium developments can be found in most metropolitan and resort areas. The condominium concept was initially utilized in high-rise residential apartments, but soon was applied to garden apartments, resort communities, and commercial office space. Today, one finds numerous condominium applications in all areas of development which can be best categorized by the following areas; the residential area, the resort area, and lastly, the commercial area. Each area is given individual attention in the descriptions below.

The residential condominium

The residential condominium continues to be the most popular offering among condominium types and is most often found in either the metropolitan or suburban areas. Within the city limits, one finds the residential condominium in the form of a modern high rise apartment building, a three to five-story new mid-rise building, or a converted older building that was formerly rental apartments. In some metropolitan condominiums, the street level floor is owned jointly by the condominium association of unit-owners and is rented out to retailers to help offset the common maintenance fees. In other cases where permitted by the state condominium statute, the retail space is sold to retailers as condominiums, or may be retained by the developer for income purposes.

In contrast to the intown condominiums, suburban condominiums are most often found in the form of garden apartments (a group of apartment buildings surrounding a common green), or cluster housing (groups of multi-unit structures usually housing 2–4 condominium units apiece each with their own private entranceway). Both forms make maximum use of the land while creating exceptional views, private entranceways, and common recreational facilities for the use of all owners; i.e., swimming pools, tennis courts, sauna baths, conference and game rooms, etc.

Some condominium developments have gone as far as offering a whole new way of life, by making available to the condominium owner all the conveniences of life. Some of these conveniences are shopping centers, restaurants, entertainment and recreational facilities, and care facilities for older persons, all of which bring the condominium community together. On the other hand, a suburban condominium may be nothing more than a series of single family homes all utilizing the same common land and parking areas.

The resort condominium

Condominium development in resort areas has grown significantly in the past few years. Resort condominiums are being built in ski country, in island resort areas, on sea coasts, and on lake shores. In the warmer climate resort areas, condominium complexes are generally built around a common recreational facility that can be enjoyed by all owners, i.e., lake, marina, seashore, golf course, island coast, etc. The condominium building itself may range from cluster housing to high-rise towers overlooking the sea.

In winter resort areas, condominiums are being built near popular ski resort areas or in some of the newer planned recreational developments. They are usually constructed in the form of town houses (built side by side); modular housing (housing constructed by standardized units placed together into various multi-unit configurations); or cluster housing. Many such winter resort condominiums also take advantage of the summer season by offering such recreational facilities as tennis courts, swimming pools, and even golf courses.

The commercial condominium

The commercial condominium, although relatively unknown to many, has unlimited potential for use in the commercial office space area. Ownership of an office condominium is very similar to the ownership of a residential condominium. The commercial condominium owner (professional, businessman, or business concern) owns his particular office space plus an undivided percentage interest in all common elements of the building. He may finance his office as he sees fit, is responsible for taxes on his own unit only, and must pay a proportionate share of the buildings overall maintenance fee.

The commercial condominium concept has been primarily used in smaller office buildings where each occupant owns a portion of each floor for his own business or profession. The most popular form of this office use is the medical or dental condominium where each doctor or dentist owns his own suite and shares such services as central answering and reception services. Often, the street level of such medical or dental condominiums are sold to retail outlets such as pharmacies, x-ray or laboratory service groups, restaurants, etc.

Another example of office condominiums is the lawyer's condominium where each lawyer or law firm owns a particular office space or entire floor. The concept has also been utilized by large banking concerns who have built downtown commercial buildings in which they occupy only the lower floors and sell the upper floors under the condominium concept.

The concept has been extended into large shopping centers and industrial parks where each business concern owns its own particular building but shares the common areas such as parking, land, sidewalks, and greens.

It becomes evident that the condominium concept can be applied to the commercial field in various forms, and is limited only by one's lack of imagination.

IV. Benefits of Condominium Living

Condominium living is here to stay. Offered is a new way of life, to the apartment dweller, to the single family home owner, and even to the professional man. For the first time, ownership is being made available in favorable metropolitan and resort areas at prices which are reasonable. This is made possible through the sharing of land and building costs by the many individual unit owners.

But what are the real benefits of condominium ownership? Are there advantages in owning a condominium rather than owning a single family home? Renting an apartment? Renting a business office? Who's buying condominiums and why?— These are questions that all potential condominium owners are asking. To help answer these questions, the following section individually analyzes the three main types of condominiums for their own special appeal.

Why buy a residential condominium?

The residential condominium can be most easily analyzed by separating the city condominium from the suburban condominium.

The metropolitan condominium

The metropolitan condominium has effectively created a new life for those who formerly rented city apartments. Those found to be most interested in metropolitan condominiums are young couples seeking home ownership, and confirmed city dwellers seeking tax shelters while enjoying the social advantages of the city. For the first time, these people can enjoy the advantages of building equity, fighting inflation through sales value appreciation, and deducting all tax and interest payments from their taxable income (discussed more fully in the financial section). They have found that through condominium ownership, adjacent condominium owners are no longer viewed as transients, but as neighbors, who wish to create a more favorable living environment. Organized work parties, social get-togethers, and helpful cooperation are not uncommon under condominium ownership. Remodeling of one's apartment is for the first time worthwhile, as is improving the image of the building through added furnishings in entranceways and lobbies. Quality maintenance and upkeep is again a requirement instead of a lost hope. And finally, although the condominium owner must now deal with rising taxes and maintenance fees, he has effectively eliminated the landlord's profit and spiraling rents.

The metropolitan condominium also offers an alternative to the suburban home owner who seeks the cultural advantages of city living. In many cases, couples whose children have grown older are now moving back into the cities to become involved in cultural activities while still enjoying the benefits of home ownership.

The suburban condominium

In contrast to the metropolitan condominium, the suburban condominium offers a new way of life mainly to single family home owners. Offered is a life free from maintenance responsibility, with the added advantage of common recreational facilities such as tennis courts, swimming pools, sauna baths, etc. The suburban condominium owner also enjoys the services of the building security personnel during his absences which are made available through the shared system of fees. For these reasons, many leisure-minded persons have left their homes to enjoy the advantages of condominium living. Older couples have also shown considerable interest in the suburban condominium due to maintenance-free living and community activities offered as previously discussed.

A third potential market for suburban condominiums is found in suburbanites who rent apartments. Although they would prefer the privacy of a single family home, due to a lack of sufficient funds, they are unable to buy. The suburban condominium, often more modestly priced than a single family home, is the answer to their desire to buy.

Why buy a resort condominium?

The resort condominium not only offers the opportunity of owning a second home in a popular resort area, but also offers the potential of a fine investment. The condominium concept has made such resort homes available at reasonable prices, with the added advantage of year-round maintenance services. No longer must one be concerned with the upkeep requirements of a second home, for such maintenance is most often carried out by an independent management company.

One other important advantage to resort condominium ownership is the potential of rental income. By renting out the condominium when not in use, one can sometimes significantly offset one's expenses. There are basically four ways in which condominium owners can rent out their condominiums; first by themselves where each owner makes his own rental arrangements, second through the assistance of a local real estate agent, third through the assistance of the condominium management company that is on an honor system to offer all available condominiums equally, and fourth, through a "rental pool" arrangement where all owners form together to offer their units for rent. Obviously, there are advantages and disadvantages to each method. The first three methods lend themselves more to part time rentals whereas the "rental pool" organization lends itself more to year-round rentals.

Because rental pools are becoming more and more popular in resort condominium offerings, it is important that the concept be well understood. The rental pool is most often managed for a fee by a professional rental agency that provides all rental services. Examples of these services are guest solicitations, rental administration, monetary management, cleaning services, and linen services. The condominium owners that participate in the rental pool each receive their proportionate share of the total income, whether or not their unit was rented as often as some others. Of course, this does not apply for the weeks that one's unit is not available for rent. This system offers the advantages of an income which offsets the ownership expenses without the burden of arranging for one's own rentals. But such rental services are expensive and often the rental agency tends to over-exaggerate the potential rental income of one's condominium. It is therefore important that the purchase of a resort condominium not be based totally on the projected income potential. Such income should be viewed as an added benefit of resort condominium ownership. It should be noted that the federal government now requires that rental resort developments fall under the securities law as the developers are basically selling an investment opportunity. Such rental pool offerings therefore require a written prospectus of the offering to be made available to the prospective investor. (See Appendix D for additional information.)

The appeal of resort condominiums is widespread and consequently spans from the young investor who rents out his unit year-round, to the suburban homeowner who enjoys the unit with his family on weekends and rents it to his friends during the week at minimal cost. By renting the condominium out, one not only receives an income to help offset the expenses before taxes, but also receives additional deductions (maintenance expenses, operating expenses, depreciation) when computing income taxes.

It can obviously be seen that the potential of a fine investment is available through the ownership of a resort condominium. But because tax regulations differ for part-time rental and full-time rental condominiums, and quality differs so radically between offerings, it is imperative that each rental resort condominium offering be closely analyzed as further discussed in the financial section.

Why buy a commercial condominium?

The office condominium has opened up a whole new environment to all businessmen and professionals. Never before has the doctor, lawyer, or businessman had the opportunity to purchase his own office in a multi-unit office building. The development of office condominiums is presently at its highest level since the enactment of the condominium legislation in 1961. Due to the fact that there is virtually no competition in the commercial office area, which differs from residential condominiums competing with single family homes and cooperative housing, the potential of office condominiums is overwhelming.

Owning condominium office space is often less expensive than renting due to the increased federal tax shelter through the use of the depreciation deduction. All income-producing properties, in this case office space, can be depreciated over a reasonable time span for federal income tax purposes. Under the rental situation, the landlord benefits by depreciation, where as under condominium ownership, the condominium office owner benefits from the depreciation. This yearly depreciable amount may be deducted from the office condominium owner's taxable federal income, thereby resulting in a lower federal tax. The office condominium owner may also deduct his mortgage expenses from his taxable federal income. Although the rental tenant has the right to deduct all rental costs and business expenses, these deductions are comparable to the mortgage, real estate tax, and maintenance deductions under condominium ownership. The main advantage of ownership over rental then is the additional depreciation deduction allowable under condominium ownership. (Such deductions are further explained in the financial section.)

The office condominium owner also enjoys the added benefits of equity growth, resale value appreciation, and the security that any change in interior design and installation of equipment is protected over the long run. Another important area to be considered in office condominium ownership is the control factor which is inherent in the association of unit owners. The owners have the power to determine what use restrictions they wish to place on the building. For instance, the doctor-owners of a medical condominium may restrict the use of the building to medical purposes only. They may provide themselves with a right to purchase any unit being offered for resale. And most important, the condominium owners have the power to control the way in which the building is managed, thereby eliminating the problems of unsatisfactory maintenance work.

One area often seen as a drawback in office condominium ownership is the inflexibility of future expansion. But when compared to the typical rental situation of being surrounded by long-term lease tenants, this flexibility seems inevitable in any case. If a move is required, the condominium owner at least has the flexibility to either lease or sell his space, and need not get involved in the penalty costs of breaking long-term lease agreements.

Conclusion

It can be concluded that the various types of condominiums obviously attract particular segments of the population, and, in general, offer to those particular segments many ownership advantages. But before one proceeds to the analysis section of this buyer's guide, it is important that the alternative to condominium ownership is clearly understood, that of *cooperative ownership.*

V. What About Cooperative Ownership?

The question of how cooperatives differ from condominiums invariably arises in discussions concerning condominium ownership. Because of wide misunderstanding on this subject, the following section deals specifically with the major similarities and differences between the two forms of ownership.

Definition of cooperative ownership

In a cooperative building, the owners own the building as a group, generally through a corporation, with each owner owning a number of shares of stock in proportion to the value of his apartment. Each apartment is consequently leased from the corporation under a so-called proprietary lease. The mortgage covers the entire property with each owner paying his proportionate share. The owners also pay their proportionate share of the property tax and the maintenance cost for the building as a whole.

Similarities of condominiums & cooperatives

The forms of ownership are similar insofar as they both offer the same benefits as owning a single family home. Both forms allow one to deduct all property taxes and mortgage interest payments from one's taxable income. In the case of the cooperative, such benefits are available under provisions of the Internal Revenue Code which allow the individual cooperative shareholder to deduct his proportionate share of the corporation's property taxes and mortgage interest payments. But these provisions require that 80% of the cooperative shareholders hold leases within the building, in order to gain such benefits. However, they do not restrict the lease holders from subleasing their cooperative apartments. Both forms of ownership provide equity growth, value appreciation, and management control.

28

Differences between condominiums & cooperatives

The differences between condominium ownership and cooperative ownership can best be shown by comparisons in the following three areas:

Financial Dependency
Flexibility of Resale
Design Flexibility

Financial dependency

As previously discussed, condominium ownership offers individual unit financing, as well as individual unit tax assessment. Only the maintenance fees are shared with other unit owners. In the case of the cooperative, all expenses are shared. It is therefore most important that each cooperative owner pay his share of the expenses each month, otherwise, any unpaid expenses would have to be supported by the remaining owners. Any unpaid financing fees could cause a default of the single mortgage thereby causing a loss of all cooperative apartments. Such financial dependency is minimized under the condominium form of ownership due to the individualized unit financing and tax assessments.

Flexibility of resale

The flexibility of resale is an important consideration in any form of ownership due to the transient nature of our society today. Such resale flexibility is more prominent under condominium ownership than under cooperative ownership due to the following two reasons. First, the effect of a condominium resale on the neighboring condominium owners is slight, due to each owner's financial independency (individual mortgage and tax payments). This, of course, is not the case under the cooperative form of ownership, where there is a considerable financial dependency between owners, therefore requiring a more formal scrutiny of prospective cooperative owners. But second and most important is the fact that the cooperative owner cannot offer a new financing package with a low cash payment to the prospective purchaser. Each new purchaser of a cooperative is held to the terms of the original single mortgage. If the original loan on the single mortgage has been reduced by 50%, the new cooperative purchaser must produce 50% of the purchase price in cash to the former cooperative owner. This must be compared with new conventional financing on single family houses or condominium units which is available in amounts up to 70%–80% of the sales value. It should be noted that personal loans on cooperatives are most often viewed as stock loans by most lending institutions, which limits the availability of long term financing. (There are exceptions to this rule; for instance, in New York State, many institutions offer long term financing for New York State cooperatives.) Under condominium ownership, the purchaser may obtain new conventional financing and therefore may reduce his initial cash requirement. This financial flexibility under condominium ownership obviously makes a condominium more salable to a larger percentage of potential buyers.

The ability to renew the financing of one's mortgage when in need of cash, called refinancing, is another important consideration. One advantage to cooperative ownership is that the cooperative owners may refinance their single mortgage for the building as a whole so that certain improvements in the central areas can be made. This is somewhat difficult under con-

dominium ownership, as all units are independently financed, if financed at all. But there is an advantage to condominium ownership which is that each individual has the ability to obtain needed cash by refinancing his separate mortgage. This, of course, is impossible for the cooperative owners, as all individu-   •
als are tied to one single mortgage.

➤ ㄱㄱ ㄱ

Design flexibility

The design flexibility within each owner's unit is the last consideration to be discussed. Although there is no rigid rule under either form of ownership which prescribes what renovations may or may not be performed within one's unit, it has been found that condominiums on the whole offer less restrictions and guidelines for renovation than do cooperatives. This is primarily due to the fact that if the cooperative owner defaults on his payments and loses his proprietary lease to his unit, it is the responsibility of the remaining cooperative owners to either sell or lease the space. If the interior of such a unit has been poorly redesigned, it will be quite difficult to sell without some renovation work. Consequently, many cooperative developments have placed restrictions on the amount of interior redesign work permitted. Under condominium ownership, the owners have full flexibility of interior design, as long as it does not interfere with the central areas or neighboring units. A poor interior design in one owner's unit has no financial effect on the other condominium owners.

In summary, condominium ownership offers the advantages of individual unit financing, individual unit tax assessment, resale flexibility, interior design flexibility, and limited dependency on the financial viability of other unit owners. The cooperative form of ownership offers none of these advantages. The flexibility of condominium ownership is obviously preferable to that of cooperative ownership. One can therefore conclude that condominiums are the wave of future multi-unit ownership.

CHOOSING THE

RIGHT CONDOMINIUM

───────────

────────────────

────────────────────────

IT HAS BECOME OBVIOUS FROM THE FIRST SECTION THAT there are many types of condominiums each with their own advantages and benefits. Choosing the type of condominium desired should be no great task, as each offers a different life style, be it a garden complex in the suburbs, a modular condominium in a ski area, or a conversion unit in the city. The difficulty arises when comparing similar offerings of the same type. It is therefore the purpose of this section to aid one in choosing the right condominium to buy, and to find out whether the investment is advisable financially.

The importance of a thorough analysis of a condominium offering cannot be over-emphasized. There is no need for misunderstanding and purchaser apprehension. Whether the condominium offering is a new offering or a resale, all documentation should be thoroughly reviewed and all features analyzed. For these reasons, the following section deals specifically with the steps and the considerations that must be taken by a condominium buyer to assure a satisfactory purchase.

The steps to be considered are reviewed in the following sequence:

1) Performance of a simplified comparative market study.

2) Review of all legal documentation for its workability.

3) Analysis of the design features for their potential resale appreciation.

4) Analysis of the management plan for its operational feasibility.

5) Review of the financial obligation for determination of its soundness.

I. Analyzing the Condominium Marketplace

The performance of a simplified market study is a must when considering the purchase of a condominium unit, due to the newness of the concept. This requires nothing more than making simple comparisons of various offerings with regard to the following areas: location, pricing, neighborhood, zoning, sales activity, and prospective purchasers. Each area of consideration is briefly reviewed below.

Location

The prime consideration in any offering is its location; how close it is to shopping areas, cultural attractions, schools, and recreational facilities. The location should also offer excellent views, ample parking, and privacy. If the location of a condominium offering is ideal, many other features can be overlooked. But if the location is undesirable, no amount of additional features will make the purchase of a unit in the condominium desirable.

Pricing

The condominium offering must be priced competitively with other similar offerings, as well as with single family homes and rental units in the surrounding neighborhood. The prices for condominiums most often run 10% to 30% less than the prices for comparable single family homes in the same neighborhood with comparable living space. In comparing prices, however, one must consider the common facilities available to the condominium owner; i.e., saunas, game rooms, tennis courts, swimming pool, etc.

When compared with similar rental units, condominium monthly costs before federal taxes run equal to or slightly higher than monthly rental costs, but somewhat less after tax savings have been taken. A general rule of thumb to use in determining the average sales price of a condominium unit is to multiply the potential yearly rent of a comparable unit by a factor of nine (9). For example, if one's apartment is offered to him for purchase, a rent of $275 per month would justify a price range of approximately $33,000, or $275 $\times$ 12 mos. $\times$ 9 = $33,000.

In high rise condominiums, prices vary substantially depending on the location and view; for instance, in elevator buildings, prices increase at a rate of 1% to 3% as one moves up from floor to floor, but may vary up to 20% within a floor strictly due to view or noise considerations. In three story walkups, prices for third floor units are found to be 5% to 15% lower than first and second levels.

The sales price per square foot for condominiums generally fall under three separate price ranges, $18–$23 per sq. ft. for moderate accommodations, $24–$35 per sq. ft. for better accommodations, and $36–$60 per sq. ft. for exceptional accommodations. The figures vary within each range depending on land and building costs, the location, and the amenities offered.

In the case of a resale, find out when the original offering was made and at what price. Then by using an appropriate sales value appreciation rate per year for the neighborhood (1% to 6%), determine the appropriate maximum resale price. If the offering price far exceeds the figure calculated by using the appropriate appreciation rate, don't purchase the condominium until such a value can be justified. For instance, what additions, if any, have been made? An offering price equal to the original sales price or only slightly higher indicates trouble, either in the neighborhood, the building, or in the original pricing structure.

Neighborhood

The status of the surrounding community is an important consideration to the condominium buyer. If the neighborhood is improving, there should be little trouble selling the condominium at an appreciated price in the near future. On the other hand, if the neighborhood is deteriorating, the resale value of the condominium may be less than the original sales value. It is therefore important that one should learn as much as possible about the neighboring buildings, houses, and shopping areas. For instance, have the single family homes been selling at substantially appreciated prices; have the apartments had vacancy problems, and has the shopping center been expanding? The school system should also be checked in the case of a residential condominium. By just looking into these few areas of consideration, much can be learned about the condition and direction of the neighborhood.

Zoning

The zoning of adjacent lots should be checked to make certain that projects of an offensive nature cannot be built. A local zoning map, available at city halls, will immediately show which areas are zoned for business, which areas are zoned for multi-unit residential housing, and which areas are planned for single family homes.

It is also important to make sure that no new buildings are planned for construction which would limit one's privacy and view. Other areas to check are the noise and disturbance factors from overhead plane routes, bus and train lines, and commuter automobile traffic.

Sales activity

Much can be learned from the different levels of sales activity of new condominium offerings. A successful condominium project is one in which there is a high level of sales activity resulting in a quick sellout of all condominium units. This kind of activity can mean much to the condominium owner. First, this activity means that there is continued market interest in the condominium project. Such interest creates a favorable resale market which can substantially appreciate resale prices. It also assures that the maintenance budget will be supported by a full contingency of unit owners.

On the other hand, a low level of activity during a sales promotion often indicates trouble. The project may be poorly located, overpriced, or just lacking in appeal. One must be very cautious in the purchase of a unit in such an offering, for even if the best unit in the condominium is purchased, there is no guarantee that the other units will be sold and that the building will be declared a condominium.

It is a common practice for a developer of a condominium to reserve the right in the condominium units' purchase and sale agreement to cancel the agreement if a stated minimum number of units are not sold within a stated time period. The reason for reserving this right is that it may not be financially possible or feasible to "condominiumize" the project unless the stated minimum number of units is sold. Even if enough units are sold and the building is declared a condominium, the units that haven't sold may have to be rented by the developer to support the financing of the building. This lessens the chance for the condominium owners to control their building and often discourages future sales due to the transient nature of the rental tenants.

It is therefore important to review the sales progress and activity of any offering by asking the following simple questions:

How long has the offering been on the market?

How many units have been sold?

Have purchase and sale agreements been signed on the

sold units, or have these units just been reserved?

Have the original prices changed?

Which units are selling?

By learning the answers to the above questions and by noticing the activity in the sales office, one should be in a better position to analyze the offering. If the condominium offering has been on the market for more than nine months and has only ½ of the units sold, watch out! It is also important to understand the commitment of purchase, for if the units indicated as sold are merely reserved, by letters of intention or the like, the solidarity of the offering must be questioned. Also watch out if the prices for the units have been lowered to increase sales. Stable or slightly rising prices generally indicate a successful venture. The last area to check is the location of the units already sold. If they are all on the side of the building with the view, that doesn't say much for the project as a whole. Also if they are all the lower priced units, or all the two bedroom units, it indicates a sales problem for the remainder of the building. If the units sold are evenly distributed throughout the building, it can be assumed that the building has the potential for a sellout.

Much can also be learned from the techniques used by the condominium sales personnel. Some sales techniques to note can be seen in the following examples:

1) The salesman who offers anything and everything. (The project is most probably in need of sales.)

2) The salesman who answers all specific questions with: Don't worry about it; it is unimportant. (The project has been poorly conceived and planned. Indicates the potential for future problems.)

3) The salesman who always has the perfect unit, and luckily,

it happens to be the last unit available. Take it or leave it. (In most cases, such a technique indicates a lack of interest for the purchaser's welfare, which is often an indication of things to come. Also interesting is the fact that the "last unit available" never seems to really be the last unit.)

4) The salesman who shows you the various offerings available, but also notes that the condominium has certain restrictions (no pets) and a limited number of design options. (This technique indicates that the development is well planned, and that the salesman has confidence that the project will sell itself.)

Although the analysis of such sales techniques can be helpful in analyzing the offering as a whole, it must be understood that certain sales techniques may be representative of only the individual salesman and not the offering as a whole.

Prospective purchasers

The last area to be reviewed concerns the potential purchaser. Who is the potential buyer for a specific offering? This is an important question, for obviously a young single man or woman would feel uneasy living in a building filled with retirees. And vice versa. This, of course, is an extreme example, but it is advisable to determine the type of buyer that has been showing interest in a particular offering. Finding out what the restrictions are on the offering will also give one an idea of who will be living in his building—families or singles, older people, or younger people. Ask, for example, if there is a restriction on children under 16 or pets.

Summary

The questions in this section, Analyzing the Condominium Market, should aid the purchaser considerably in determining the feasibiliy of the project today and its resale potential for the future.

II. What to Look for in the Legal Documents

The overall review of the legal documents is the responsibility of a qualified lawyer so that the potential purchaser is assured protection. But this is not to say that the purchaser should not understand the documents and the offering plan himself. By knowing what documents to review and what questions to ask, the purchaser can better analyze the offering and determine its creditability. (See Sample Legal Documents in Appendix C).

Document definitions

The types of documents that the purchaser should be familiar with are the following:

> The Purchase and Sale Agreement
> The Master Deed or Declaration
> The Unit Deed
> The Bylaws
> The Regulations

These documents are briefly defined in sequence below and will then be analyzed from the purchaser's viewpoint. It should be noted that in order for a building to be officially declared a condominium, the state statutes require that the master deed, unit deed, and by-laws be recorded at the registry of deeds.

Purchase and sale agreement

The purchase and sale agreement is the legal document of sale which stipulates the selling and buying parties, the unit to be purchased, the sale price of the unit, the deposit required, the delivery date of the unit deed, the financial arrangements, and any contingencies of sale. Such contingencies may include a provision for cancellation of the purchase and sale agreement if the seller is unable to sell a stated number of units.

The master deed (declaration)

The master deed is required to commit the land to condominium use. Included is a description of the land, the building(s), the units within the building(s), and the common areas, the measurements of all of which must be certified by a registered engineer. Each unit's proportionate interest in the common areas and facilities is generally set forth on an attached schedule. A statement of the building's purpose and use is defined and the type of organization that will manage the condominium is indicated.

The unit deed

The unit deed describes each of the units specifically as to size, location, and use, and is ordinarily recorded at the time of delivery to the unit buyer.

The bylaws

Bylaws are also required to be recorded with the Master Deed, and, in general, cover the establishment of the unit-owner's board of managers, the guidelines by which the unit-owners are elected to the board, and the standards by which they must rule. This management organization may be set up in the form of a trust, corporation or association. In many cases, a trust is formed in which the personnel of the development company initially act as trustees on the management board. These trustee positions are eventually turned over to the unit-owners through official elections as the condominium building nears sellout. Many of the operating procedures for the condominium's management board are described in the bylaws. Methods for collecting maintenance assessments, rules for maintenance work, repair work, and replacement, and systems for hiring of personnel are some of these operating procedures described.

Regulations

A list of regulations is ordinarily attached to, or included in, the bylaws which define general guidelines for living in the condominium complex. They are drawn up to protect the desired image of the condominium community, and to aid in the condominium's operations. These guidelines can be altered by a majority vote, whereas amendments to the master deed and the bylaws generally require a two-thirds vote.

Document analysis

In this analysis section, each of the documents will be discussed from the purchaser's point of view. The importance of these documents cannot be over-emphasized, as they indicate the working plan of the development and the overall plans of the developer and management company. Because many of the new condominiums being sold on the market have not been officially declared, the only way to view the condominium as it will be is through the proposed documents.

Purchase and sale agreement

The following review includes pertinent questions with respect to the Purchase and Sale documentation. Also included in this review are statements relating to the temporary reservation of a unit while analyzing the offering. All such questions must be thoroughly understood before the signing of any condominium purchase and sales agreement.

1) If a deposit is required to temporarily reserve a unit for further inspection, is the deposit returnable upon request?
2) If a firm deposit is placed on a particular unit, is the deposit being placed in an escrow account for the protection of the buyer, and will the escrow account bear interest for the buyer?
3) Is the declaration date of the development specifically defined, so that it is understood when the building will officially become a condominium?
4) If a specific number of units have not been signed for by a specific date, can one request that his initial deposit be returned? This is an important consideration, for the prospective purchaser should not be bound to a failing development.
5) Has it been clarified that the deposit money will not be used for any construction purposes until the condominium project has reached a satisfactory level of unit sales?
6) If not declared a condominium due to the lack of sufficient sales, are there any rental arrangements anticipated? This will be important to those persons who will have committed to move from their present housing arrangements.
7) If forced into a temporary rental situation due to a delayed declaration of the condominium, will the monthly rental

costs be applied to the anticipated condominium purchase price?

8) Has the developer made arrangements for long term financing of condominium units?

9) Are all financial obligations clearly spelled out and understood? Reservation deposits, initial cash payments, mortgage payments, taxes, and maintenance fees.

10) Most important, has a lawyer reviewed the agreement from the purchaser's viewpoint, and found it acceptable?

The master deed

The following questions are pertinent when reviewing the master deed, or declaration of the condominium offering.

1) Are the common facilities/ elements of the condominium offering well defined, and are all such elements to be owned by the unit owners? For example, in some offerings, developers have retained certain common elements, such as parking areas or recreational facilities and charge an additional monthly fee for their use. There are also common elements that may have contingencies that require further explanation; for example, a swimming pool and bathhouse that will eventually be shared with a second complex of buildings: Question—How will the monthly maintenance fees be adjusted when the new owners participate?

2) Is the condominium a leasehold condominium where the land is to be retained by the developer or a third party? If so, it is important to understand the terms and restrictions of the lease, and make certain that the term is infinite in nature so as to protect future owners.

3) Has the developer or contractor offered warranties on the various facilities of the building and the appliances? In new construction, most equipment, appliances, and building materials are warranteed for a certain time period, so that the new unit owner will not be liable for obvious construc-

tion, or manufacturing fault. In older buildings, central facitities such as wiring, plumbing, heating systems and roofing should be warranteed for a period of one year or more if not initially renovated by the developer.

4) Is the description of the unit adequate, so that when the building is completed and ready for occupancy, it is the same unit that was anticipated? For example, the appliances must be specified, the room dimensions and ceiling heights detailed, the construction materials stipulated, and all carpets, wall coverings, and cabinet work defined.

5) Is each owner's percentage of ownership clearly defined? This is important as the percentage determines the monthly maintenance fee. (Unit Owner's Maintenance Fee/Yr.) = (Percentage Ownership × Building Maintenance Budget-/Yr.) Even more important is the fact that if the building is destroyed, or dissolved by unanimous vote, the percentage ownership factor determines the reimbursement figure to each owner. The following table shows how the percentage ownership is determined:

Floor	Unit	Initial Sales Price	Percentage Ownership
1	A	$ 40,000	20%
1	B	50,000	25%
2	A	50,000	25%
2	B	60,000	30%
		$200,000	100%

$$\frac{\text{Percentage}}{\text{Ownership}} \ (\text{Unit 1A}) = \frac{\text{Initial Sales Price}}{\text{Total Aggregate Sales}} = \frac{\$40,000}{\$200,000} = 20\%$$

It must be understood that at the time of declaration, the recorded percentages are the final percentages, even if the unsold units eventually sell for more or less than originally declared. For example, if three out of the four units are sold and the deeds are recorded, the unsold unit (say 2A) continues to hold the same percentage ownership of 25%. If the developer exercised his right to lower the $50,000 price to $40,000 in order to help sell the unit, the new percentage ownership would seem to be $40,000 ÷ $200,000 or 20%. But this is not the case, as all percentages at recordation are frozen to protect the present owners. Only by a unanimous vote by all the unit owners can these percentages be changed.

6) Does the "use description" of the building meet with the purchaser's requirements? For instance, is it possible for a business enterprise to move in next door, or is the building restricted to residential use? Make sure that one's plans coincide with the "use description" so as to be assured adequate protection.

The bylaws

When reviewing the bylaws, make certain that the following questions have been answered:

1) What type of organization has the developer chosen to manage the condominium; trust, association, or corporation; and at what point does the developer plan to turn over control to the unit owner?

If the offering is a new building, it is found that most developers will initially retain control of the management through one of the above organizations (trust, association, or corporation) in order to assure that the image of the offering is adequately maintained while selling the remaining unsold units. Upon reaching a certain percentage of sales, or by reaching a specified date, most developers turn control over to the unit owners, so that they may maintain the property as they see fit. An example of such a turnover policy might read as follows: "On November 31, 1974, or when 75% of all condominium units are sold, whichever

47

shall first occur, the Developer shall notify all unit owners thereof, and the first annual meeting of unit owners shall be held so that officers may be elected."

2) What maintenance arrangements has the developer made so as to assure quality maintenance upkeep? What is the term of the agreement?

Be certain that the management company hired is well qualified in the field of management. It is also important to find out whether the management contract can be renegotiated after a year's period, for sometimes developers guarantee themselves extensive management contracts, and thereby limit the unit owners' privilege of selecting their own management group.

3) Is the insurance coverage adequate to cover the building for fire, theft and liability?

It is important that such insurance is adequate, so as to protect the condominium association against loss from fire damage, burglary, or personal suits. It should also be noted that the master policy for a condominium does not cover the possessions in one's unit, therefore requiring additional policies for full protection.

The regulations

The regulations that are attached to, or included in, the bylaws *vary* according to the special needs and desires of each group of condominium owners. Make certain that such regulations are acceptable before signing any binding agreements. Some of the more common regulations that are most often found are as follows:

1) All children's play is restricted to the play area in the rear of the building, and under no circumstances may children play in the public halls, elevators, stairways or entranceways.

48

2) All common areas, such as hallways, stairways, walkways, and entranceways must be kept unobstructed so as to allow proper ingress to and egress from the apartment building.

3) No articles may be hung or shaken from any terraces or windows of the condominium.

4) No bicycles, wagons, scooters or similar vehicles may be stored in the public areas.

5) Owners are not permitted to make disturbing noises, which interfere with the rights, comforts, and conveniences of other unit owners.

6) No cooking shall be permitted on any of the terraces unless permission has been granted by the board of managers.

7) No articles may be stored in the basement, except where stipulated by the board of managers.

8) A key to each unit must be retained by the board of managers, and any alteration to the lock must be under the consent of the board of managers. If consent is given for the alteration, the board of managers must be provided with a new key.

9) Any complaints in reference to the maintenance service must be reported in written form to the board of managers.

10) No cats or dogs may be kept in the condominium. All other pets must be confined to the unit-owner's apartment, as long as they in no way annoy neighboring apartment owners.

Summary

By reviewing the various legal documents as discussed in this chapter, one can certainly gain a better insight into the condominium being offered. But it is important to understand that a thorough analysis of such documents should be performed by a qualified real estate lawyer if purchasing a condominium.

III. What Design Features to Check

The design features of a condominium development can make the difference between a salable project and an unsalable one. And more importantly, the features have much to do with the rate at which the units may appreciate in value. It is therefore imperative that the following areas of design be considered when analyzing a condominium offering.

> Project Image
> Amenities
> Common Facilities
> Parking

Project image

The appeal of a condominium offering is of prime importance. The attractiveness of the setting is as critical as the building design itself. A conscious effort by the developer and architect to create such a favorable setting can make the difference between a salable unit and an unsalable one. For instance, in the landscaping area, has the builder planted a few trees and some shrubbery, or has he made a real effort to create a more luxurious image with varied walkways, benches, ground swells, lighting, larger trees, hedges, etc.? Has the architect also situated the parking areas so as not to interfere with condominium or roadside views?

In the area of design, has privacy been protected through the use of private entrances or courtyards? If common entrances are utilized, are they appealing, spacious, and comfortable? And has the overall architectural plan produced a satisfying projection of lines, angles, and curves? Often, varied rooflines and entranceways create the needed appeal.

In all cases, visualize the condominium as it will be when all units are occupied; i.e., parking lots full, activity of people, noise, swimming pool activity, additional clusters of housing, etc. This should help in analyzing the project's real image.

Overall, it is important that this image projected by the condominium is more favorable than those of competitive projects, neighboring apartment buildings, or even neighboring single family homes.

Amenities

It is often stated that condominiums offer the same amenities as single family homes with the added advantage of shared common facilities such as saunas, community rooms, swimming pool, gardens, etc. It is therefore quite helpful to analyze a condominium offering from the viewpoint one would use in considering a single family home. In essence, does the condominium unit offer the same amenities offered in the single family home?

A check list has been compiled below which should help the purchaser in analyzing the amenities offered:

1) Is the electricity, gas, and heat metered individually as in the single family home? If not, will the sharing of such utilities be detrimental?
2) Are there interior design options available? Most significant are the designs for the kitchen and bathroom areas.
3) Are the kitchen appliances and bathroom facilities the type that one would want in his own single family home?
4) Are flues available in the kitchen to disperse fumes?
5) Are the rooms spacious, with adequate natural light and ventilation? Is air conditioning available?
6) If carpeting is available, will it be padded?

7) Are the walls adequately soundproofed so that noise from adjoining condominiums is minimized? Ample sound-proofing is also required in ceilings and floors in multi-unit buildings.
8) Is there flexibility of room use; for instance, can a den or study substitute for a guest room or baby's room?
9) Most important of all is the consideration of privacy. Is it adequate?

Common facilities

The design of the common facilities of the condominium often depict the quality of an offering. Such quality can best be determined by checking the common areas listed below:

1) The lobby should be spacious, well lighted, comfortable, and designed compatibly with the overall image of the building.
2) All public and private entrances must be adequately secured with the availability of double lock systems.
3) If a front entranceway is required, it should include a quality two way inter-com system for security purposes.
4) Service entrances must be in the rear of the building, so that service calls can be made without inconveniencing the front lobby thoroughfare.
5) The elevator must ride swiftly, smoothly, and must stop evenly with all floor stops, including lower parking levels, if any.
6) Central laundry facilities must be offered, either centrally or individually, as well as community rooms, saunas, locker rooms, and individual storage spaces in the basement.
7) Such common facilities as elevators, laundry rooms, and game rooms should be so located so as to not interfere with nearby units.
8) Garbage and trash removal facilities must be made available, as well as proper property drainage systems.

In order to properly evaluate such common facilities, each

facility must be checked for its practical usage. For instance, an offering may indicate the availability of central laundry facilities, but might have only three machines available for 50 unit owners. In the same way, storage space may be offered, but after researching the matter, only a 4 ft. $\times$ 5 ft. space is available.

Larger recreational facilities, such as tennis courts or swimming pools should definitely be researched. The size and depth of the pool and the number and type of tennis courts will help to further describe such facilities. It is also important to determine the time schedule on constructing such facilities for they are usually the lowest construction priority.

Parking

Parking availability has been singled out as a prime design consideration due to its importance to most home owners. First, make certain that the parking facility is a part of the condominium offering, and that it offers adequate space for both unit owners and guests. The parking facility should be a short walking distance from any unit, yet so situated that it does not detract from the project's image.

Often builders place garages between the main structures to break up the rooflines or construct separate garaging facilities with the same materials as the main structures. Both techniques help improve the project's appeal while making parking available. Parking availabilty is especially important in the intown condominiums for its availability can substantially appreciate resale values.

Summary

In summary, the design features of a condominium have much influence on a project's acceptability as well as on its potential to appreciate in value. By analyzing the design features as indicated in the above areas, it will soon become evident which offering has best considered the purchaser's needs.

IV. Analyzing the Management Function

The assurance of continued satisfaction in a condominium ownership plan depends heavily on the expertise of the management company. The initial management company is most often contracted by the developer to carry out the management function of the condominium. Such management contracts will eventually be negotiated by the unit owners themselves, but until such power has been turned over to them, each owner must accept the present management arrangements. It is therefore important that the management company be experienced in managing condominiums and be highly regarded by the community and the local municipal authorities, i. e., Chamber of Commerce, Better Business Bureau, banks, etc.

Responsibility of the management company

The responsibility of properly managing a condominium development is significant. Included in the responsibilities are such duties as projection of budgets, collection services, maintenance and cleaning services, security services, and even communication services with the unit owners through a monthly management letter. Each service must be well defined and budgeted, for the payment of the total management cost is the responsibility of the unit owners through the vehicle of a maintenance fee.

Such budget projections should be based on previous operating figures, yet in the case of a new offering where previous costs are unavailable, estimates by a professional management company are a must. In many offerings without professional management consultation, maintenance fee projections are underestimated in order to assist sales. It is therefore imperative that one finds out exactly what is to be included in the maintenance fee and what costs are projected.

Definition of services

The management services offered under the monthly maintenance fee can vary significantly from one development to the next. Such services are generally costed under the following four categories: Operational and maintenance costs, management costs, fixed costs, reserve costs. It is most important that such cost areas are defined for a condominium's yearly operational and maintenance budget.

Operational and Maintenance Costs

Utilities (Electricity, gas, oil,)
Heating costs
Sewer and water costs
Janitorial and cleaning services
Trash and garbage disposal services
Ground and building maintenance services
Window washing services

Snow removal services
Swimming pool maintenance and security
Security services—doormen, etc.

Management Costs

Legal and accounting services
Management fee
Other management costs

Fixed Costs

Building insurance
Elevator maintenance
Other fixed costs

Reserve Costs

Reserve for unexpected repair work
Reserve for replacement of common area
carpets, furniture, etc.
Reserve for improvements and alterations
to common facilities
Other reserve funds

Summary

One can see the importance of the management role. And because, in most cases, the developer will choose the initial management company, it is again important to know the developer's reputation as well as that of the management company's.

V. Financial Considerations

The importance of understanding the financial obligation of condominium ownership cannot be overemphasized. Because the final decision of purchase is always a financial one, it is mandatory that various financial obligations be fully analyzed so that an intelligent decision can be made.

An overall analysis of condominium financing becomes quite complex due to the various types of condominium offerings. For this reason, the three distinct types of condominium have each been singled out for analysis:

1) The residential condominium
2) The resort condominium
3) The commercial condominium

But before the above types of condominiums are analyzed, it is imperative that the financial obligations of home ownership in general are understood because condominium ownership is simply one form of home ownership. One will be in a better position to analyze the advantages and disadvantages of condominium ownership if general home ownership obligations are first reviewed using the example of the single family home. Many readers of this guide will already have been home owners and this will be a familiar ground of departure for a consideration of condominium ownership obligations.

General Ownership Responsibilities

The responsibilites of home ownership are many, yet so are the benefits. In the following section such responsibilities and benefits are discussed in detail so as to familiarize the reader with the ownership terms to be used in subsequent sections. The ownership responsibilities to be discussed include the initial cash investment, the mortgage obligations, the property tax payments, and the maintenance payments. The ownership benefits discussed include the various tax benefits, the equity growth, and value appreciation potential.

To best describe such general home ownership responsibilities, an example of single family home ownership will be used as presented below.

Financing a Single Family Home

The most important investment decision in many people's lives is the purchase of a single family home. It is therefore important that one not only understand ownership responsibilities, but also understand why ownership is superior to renting.

In the following section, the financial responsibilities of a single family home are first described in general terms, then in detailed terms, and are eventually compared to the option of renting comparable space.

A General Description of Financing a Single Family Home

The financial responsibilities of single family home ownership are most effectively shown through the use of a cost sheet as detailed on page 71.

Assumed on the cost sheet is a purchase price of $35,000 for the single family home of which a certain portion may be financed by a bank and the rest would be required in cash.

The ownership costs are first shown before federal income taxes have been computed, and then shown after such taxes have been computed. Before taxes, the out-of-pocket costs include the principal and interest mortgage payments, the real estate taxes, and the maintenance costs. After taxes, the cost effectively equals the above out-of-pocket costs, less any tax savings and equity growth (amortization savings). The tax savings are made available through the deduction of all yearly mortgage interest and real estate taxes from one's taxable income. Therefore, after tax deductions are taken, one effectively pays taxes on a lower income level, and consequently accrues a tax savings. The amortization savings are, in effect, the building of equity through the principal payments, and consequently can in the long run be viewed as an investment and not a cost. Therefore the real cost of ownership for the example shown on page 71 is $3,071.55/year. And this real cost of ownership has yet to include the potential for sales value appreciation. Such value appreciation, as well as a more detailed description of the cost sheet shown, is discussed in the following section.

Detailed Financing Considerations

A more detailed review of single family home ownership responsibilities and benefits are described below. Included in the description are the *Initial Cash Investment,* the *Monthly Ownership Expenses,* and the *Ownership Benefits.* The cost sheet on page 71 is to be used as reference material during the discussion.

Initial cash investment

Although one may pay the total purchase price of a single family home in cash, one more often attempts to minimize his initial cash payment by financing a certain percentage of the sales price through a mortgage, as explained below. The difference between the portion financed and the overall sales price determines the amount of the initial cash investment. This initial cash investment on most single family homes varies between 15% and 30% of the sales price. In the example shown on page 71, 25% of the sales price is required in cash, totaling $8,750.

Monthly ownership expenses

Ownership of a single family home generally requires the following monthly expenses; the *mortgage obligation,* the *real estate taxes,* and the *maintenance costs.*

Mortgage obligation

The portion of the purchase price that is financed through a lending institution is called the *mortgage obligation.* Such an obligation means that the property being purchased will be designated as the security for the loan until the loan is fully repaid. Generally, one can obtain mortgage financing for 60% to 85% of the purchase price of the single family home, depending on the buyer's financial stability, the tightness of the money market, and what interest rate is attached to the loan. The mortgage amount is termed the *principal* of the loan, which in the example shown equals 75% of $35,000 or $26,250. The *principal* of the loan is usually paid back over a 20 to 30 year period at an interest rate cost of 7% to 9%. Interest rates vary depending on the availability of mortgage money, but are also somewhat related to the loan percentage, i.e., a 90% loan on a property, if given, is obviously a higher risk to the bank and consequently carries a higher interest rate, 8% to 9%. In the example shown, the terms of the mortgage have been estimated at a typical interest rate of 7½% over a 25 year period.

Such mortgage terms indicate that the *principal* of the loan, $26,250, is to be paid back over a 25-year period at an interest rate of 7½%. Required will be a regular monthly payment that is to be paid each month over the 25-year period, which includes both the interest and principal payments. By checking a "Payment Table for Monthly Mortgage Loans," one can determine his monthly mortgage payment. For instance, for the $26,250 loan in the example shown, one's monthly mortgage payment is approximately $194.00 (includes both principal and interest).*

The breakdown of the interest payment and principal payment within the monthly mortgage payment is somewhat more complex. In the earlier years of the typical so-called "direct reduction" mortgage, which provides for equal monthly mortgage payments, a large percentage of the monthly payment is paid toward the interest charge, and little is paid toward the principal of the loan. In the latter years of the mortgage, a larger portion of the monthly mortgage charge is paid toward the balance of the loan (remaining principal to be paid) and little is paid toward the interest charge.

In order to show this more clearly, a banker's "loan progress chart" can be checked to determine the actual principal and interest breakdown. Such a breakdown is shown below for the

---

* Mortgage payment tables are made available in Appendix F for readers requiring monthly and yearly mortgage figures for various sized loans.

$26,250 loan indicated in the example cost sheet. The table is shown on a yearly basis, thereby portraying the $194.00 monthly mortgage cost as a yearly cost of $2,328 ($194.00 × 12 months). Also shown on the loan progress chart (amortization schedule) is the balance of the loan (remaining principal to be paid).

Loan Progress Chart
($26,250 Principal)
(7½%/25 yrs.)

Year of Mortgage	Interest Payment	Principal Payment	Yearly Payment	Balance of Loan
1	$1,961	$ 367	$2,328	$25,883
2	1,934	394	2,328	25,489
3	1,883	445	2,328	25,044
4	1,856	472	2,328	24,572
5	1,828	500	2,328	24,072
10	1,593	735	2,328	20,921
15	1,278	1,050	2,328	16,350
20	808	1,520	2,328	9,686
25	258	2,070	2,328	-0-

It becomes quite evident from examining the above chart that the interest payments are more heavily weighted in the first few years of the mortgage than the latter years and vice versa for the principal payments. In order to arrive at a usable percentage breakdown of principal and interest payments for analysis purposes, a ten-year average figure has been calculated as depicted

62

on the example cost sheet. Such an averaging technique will be explained in a further section.

It is interesting to note that after paying $2,328.00 per year for 5 years, one has only reduced the loan principal by $2,178. ($26,250 to $24,072). It is for this reason that a quick turnover of ownership is a costly operation, for little equity is built up on the first few years of ownership. What is mainly being paid off in the first few years, as seen from the chart, is the interest payment.

It is also interesting to note that on a before tax savings basis, the total cost of the mortgage seems to amount to 25 years × $2,328/yr. or $58,200. This high cost figure will be reduced by one's yearly tax savings as discussed in a further section. Also included in this high cost figure is the portion of the mortgage payment applied toward principal as a "cost" when, in reality, this principal portion is a form of savings, as will be subsequently shown.

Real estate taxes

Each single family home is assessed for property real estate taxes. The assessed value of each house is then multiplied by the local tax rate to determine the yearly property tax. Assessment systems vary from town to town, but in most cases, an assessed value is derived by taking a certain percentage of a houses's fair market value or of its most recent sales price. The tax rates per $1,000 of assessed value also vary considerably from town to town.

If the $35,000 house discussed in the example was located in a town which utilized a 75% assessment system and has a tax rate of $53 for every $1,000 of assessed value, the yearly tax could be computed by multiplying 75% times the market value of the house, times the tax rate, which equals $1,391 per year or $116 per month (75% × $35,000 × $53/$1,000.) It should also be pointed out that although the city requires that the tax be paid once near the end of each year, it is the policy of most banks to collect taxes on a monthly basis along with the mortgage payment, and in turn pay the city at the end of the year. This policy is no more than a protective device for a bank to assure that the municipal taxes are paid, for municipal liens (charge upon a property for the payment of a tax debt) have priority over mortgage liens (charge upon a property by the bank due to the non-payment of the mortgage commitment).

Maintenance costs

The cost of maintaining and running a single family home is most often more than one might expect. Although various costs are often budgeted, such as electricity, gas, oil, water, etc., there are also many hidden costs that one tends to forget. For instance, the costs expended in buying and maintaining lawn-mowers, hedge clippers, snow shovels, hand tools, etc. are often neglected in the yearly maintenance budget. Also left out are such labor costs as house painting, grass cutting, snow removal, and repair work. It is for this reason that few people really know how much it costs to maintain a home. For the $35,000 house shown in the example, a total of the above costs would run approximately $1,000 per year, or $83.33 per month.

The out-of-pocket-costs before taxes which includes the mortgage payment, the real estate taxes, and the maintenance costs, totals, in the example shown, $4,719/year or

$393.23/month. It must be remembered that such costs have not taken federal tax savings into consideration.

Ownership benefits

Understanding the benefits of ownership is the key to understanding the ownership concept. Such benefits include *federal tax savings, equity growth,* and *value appreciation.*

Tax savings

It is important to understand that home ownership provides significant federal tax savings. Such federal tax savings are made available by the lowering of one's taxable income through ownership deductions. Such ownership deductions include mortgage interest payments, and real estate taxes. The actual federal tax savings is computed by determining the difference in taxes required on one's regular taxable income and on one's reduced taxable income due to the ownership deductions.

In order to approximate such federal tax savings for purpose of analysis, one's tax bracket percentage is most often used. It is therefore imperative that the prospective purchaser know his tax bracket level. It must be understood that the tax percentage that one pays on his taxable income is less than his tax bracket percentage. This is due to the graduated system of taxes utilized by the federal government, where lower income levels are taxed at lower percentages. Therefore one's tax bracket level indicates the percentage tax required on one's last level of income. Consequently, any slight decrease of taxable income within that last level of income is taxed at the tax bracket percentage. For this reason, one's federal tax savings can be approximated by multiplying one's tax bracket percentage times the deductible amount. It must be pointed out that the correct tax bracket level to use in such calculations is the tax bracket level that relates to one's taxable income after all itemized deductions are taken; i.e.: medical expenses, contributions, gasoline, miscellaneous, and, of course, interest and taxes. One must not get caught using the tax bracket level of his gross income.

In the example shown, the allowable deductions include $1,796 of mortgage interest payments, and $1,391 of real estate taxes, totaling $3,187. Multiplying this deductible amount times one's tax bracket level ($3,187 × 35%) generates approximately $1,115.95/yr. of federal tax savings at the end of the taxable year. (Example assumes a 35% tax bracket level.)

It soon becomes evident that those with higher tax brackets receive additional federal tax savings. Highlighting this fact is the table below that compares the potential federal tax savings for persons with the following three tax bracket levels; 20%, 35%, and 50%. The cost data generated in the ownership example is used as a basis for such calculations.

The Effective Cost of Ownership
(After Federal Tax Savings)

		Tax Bracket Level		
		20%	35%	50%
Out-of-Pocket Costs Before Taxes/Yr.		$4,719	$4,719	$4,719
(Typical $35,000 Home)				
Less:				
Tax Savings through Deductions				
Mortgage Int.	$1,796			
Real Estate Tax	1,391			
Total Deductions	$3,187			
Total Tax Savings		637	1,115	1,593
(tax bracket % x deductions)				
Effective Cost After Taxes/Yr.		$4,082	$3,604	$3,126
Effective Cost After Taxes/Mo.		$ 340	$ 300	$ 260

66

The above table confirms the fact that there are additional savings available to the homeowner in a higher tax bracket. It should also be pointed out that the deductible figure used for the mortgage interest is based on an average of the first ten years of interest payments. This averaging technique is recommended due to the declining interest payment requirement from year to year (discussed in the mortgage obligation section). If the interest payment for the first year was used, $1,961, one would get an inflated picture of his potential tax savings, as the interest deduction in future years would be less. The ten-year average technique recommended assumes an ownership cycle of ten years. This technique therefore depicts a realistic cost and savings picture over that time period.

Equity growth

Home owners also benefit from equity growth through the reduction of the balance of the mortgage loan through monthly principal payments (amortization savings). Consequently, although the principal payment is one of the monthly out-of-pocket costs, it should be viewed as savings or an investment in one's home rather than a cost. In the example shown, the principal payment has been averaged over a 10-year period for the reason discussed above under Tax Savings, and realistically reduces the yearly cost by $532. But such an increase in equity growth does not affect the yearly cash requirement. Only when the house is sold will such principal payments be recovered.

The equity growth payments (principal) are most significant in the latter years of a mortgage for a greater percentage of the monthly mortgage payment is paid toward the principal balance of the loan. (See table on page 62.)

67

Value appreciation

By national standards, most houses appreciate (increase in value) at a rate of 3% to 5% per year depending on the area and economic conditions of the time. Such appreciation rates would increase the value of a $35,000 house by $1,050 to $1,750 per year. What is important to remember is that by purchasing a $35,000 house for only $8,750 cash down, one has leveraged his capital investment by a factor of 4 (i.e., $35,000 ÷ $8,750 = 4). What this means is that while one has possibly lost a 5% rate of savings bank interest on his initial cash investment, he has gained a 3% to 5% yearly rate of appreciation on the *total* sales value of his house Such appreciation in value can be significant for if the value of the property appreciates at a 5% rate each year, in 10 years the property would be valued at $57,000 which amounts to a $22,000 increase in value. Such an increase clearly overshadows the interest lost after taxes on the initial cash payment which amounts to approximately $3,582. (Assumes a 35% tax bracket level.) It should be noted that the appreciation in value is not taxable if the sales monies are reinvested in a new first home. But it must be remembered that *all* real estate does not appreciate at 3% to 5%/yr. and therefore one must carefully check the appreciation rates in the area being considered. It is not uncommon to find an area where houses values are somewhat stable, or even decrease slightly from year to year. The need to know the appreciation rates in an area cannot therefore be overemphasized.

Home Ownership Versus Rental

The most effective technique of demonstrating the benefits of home ownership is through the comparison of ownership costs versus rental costs. In order to determine a monthly rental figure for purposes of comparison, one is reminded of the formula described in the previous section, *Analyzing the Condominium Market,* that equated annual rents to potential sales values for comparable space. The formula assumed, that in a typical case, the potential sales value of a home or apartment is 9 times its annual rental potential. Therefore, for the use of comparison, a $35,000 house can be compared to a rental offering of $325/month: $$\text{Monthly rent} = \frac{\text{Purchase Price}}{9 \times 12 \text{ months}}$$

Shown on page 72 is a comparison of ownership versus rental of a comparable space. It becomes quite evident that although one must pay approximately 20% more per month under ownership before tax savings, the effective costs after tax savings are somewhat less.

To be more specific, the ownership costs/month after tax savings only, assuming a 35% tax bracket, are slightly less than rental costs; $300/month vs. $325. But one must remember that a certain amount of interest has been lost on the initial cash payment under purchase, consequently making the effective costs of ownership after tax savings and lost interest approximately the same as the cost of rental.

The main benefits of ownership are shown in the last two categories; the equity growth factor and the value appreciation factor. The principal payments being paid against the balance of the loan should be considered an investment instead of a cost and consequently effectively lower the cost of ownership to $283/month vs. $325/month for rental.

The value appreciation factor is also of prime importance in the case of resale, for it can amount to as much as 3% to 5% of the sales value per year. In the example shown, a 3% appreciation rate per year amounts to an increase in value of $1,050/year on a $35,000 house. This actually lowers the cost of ownership to $195/month versus $325/month for rental after resale.

In summary, it becomes obvious that strictly from a cash flow basis after federal taxes, the cost of maintaining a house and an apartment are somewhat comparable. It is only when one considers equity growth and value appreciation that ownership becomes truly advantageous, and then only when resale takes place. It should be noted that if a standard tax deduction is taken under the rental situation (no itemization of deductions), the effect of the tax savings through ownership will be slightly offset. But as shown by the comparative study, the advantage of ownership can be quite significant, for as summarized below, the savings through ownership of the $35,000 house described over only a ten year period can amount to $15,510. Such savings are based mainly on the equity growth and value appreciation.

Rental Cost over 10 Years	
($325/Mo. × 12 Mo. × 10 Yrs)	$39,000
Purchase Cost over 10 Years	
($2,349 × 10 Yrs)	23,490
Savings Through Ownership	$15,510

Conclusion

The knowledge of such general home ownership responsibilities and benefits is the key to understanding the financial aspects of the condominium. It therefore cannot be overemphasized that such aspects of ownership be well understood before proceeding.

Single Family Home Cost Sheet

Sales Price	$35,000	
Cash Required (25%)	$ 8,750	
Mortgage (75%)	$26,250	
Terms:	7½%–25 years	

		Yearly	Monthly
Out-of-Pocket Costs Before Taxes			
Mortgage Principal Payment (10 year average)		$ 532.00	$ 44.33
Mortgage Interest Payment (10 year average)		1,796.00	149.66
Real Estate Taxes		1,391.00	115.91
Maintenance Costs		1,000.00	83.33
		$4,719.00	$393.23
Effective Costs After Taxes			
Out-of-Pocket Costs		$4,719.00	$393.23
Less:			
Tax Savings thru Deductions			
Deductions Available:			
Mortgage Interest	$1,796		
Real Est. Taxes	1,391		
Total Deductions	$3,187		
Tax Savings (35% Bracket)		1,115.45	92.95
Effective Cost After Taxes		$3,603.55	$300.28
Less:			
Amortization Savings (Equity Growth)		532.00	44.33
Real Cost of Ownership (After Tax & Equity Considerations)		$3,071.55	$255.95

Comparison of Ownership vs. Rental

	Purchase	Rental
Sales Price	$35,000	$325/mo.
Cash Required (25%)	$8,750	
Mortgage (75%)	$26,250	
Terms 7½%-25 years		

Out-of-Pocket Costs/Before Taxes	Yearly	Monthly	Monthly
Monthly Rental Fee			$ 325
Mortgage Principal Payment (10 year average)	$ 532	$ 44	
Mortgage Interest Payment (10 year average)	1,796	150	
Real Estate Taxes	1,391	116	
Maintenance Costs	1,000	83	
Total Out-of-Pocket Costs	$4,719	$ 393	$ 325

Effective Cost After Taxes

	Yearly	Monthly	Monthly
Out-of-Pocket Costs	$4,719	$ 393	$ 325
Less:			
Tax Savings thru Deductions			
Deductions Available			
Mortgage Int. $1,796			
Real Est. Taxes 1,391			
Total Deductions $3,187			
Total Tax Savings (35% Bracket)	1,115	93	-0-
Effective Cost After Taxes	$3,604	$ 300	$ 325
Plus:			
Interest lost on $8,750 (5% rate after taxes)	+ 327	+ 27	-0-
Effective Cost After Taxes + Int. Lost	$3,931	$ 327	$ 325
Less:			
Amortization Savings (Equity Growth)	− 532	− 44	-0-
Real Cost After Taxes/Int./Equity	$3,399	$ 283	$ 325
Less:			
Appreciation in Value (3%/year)	1,050	87	-0-
Actual Cost After Resale	$2,349	$ 195	$ 325

Condominium Ownership Responsibilities

Utilizing the knowledge gained from the previous section on GENERAL OWNERSHIP RESPONSIBILITIES, one is now in the position to financially analyze the three types of condominiums: the residential condominium, the resort condominium, and the commercial condominium. As in the previous section, a sample cost sheet will be generated for each of the three types of condominiums. Such costs will then be used as a basis for analysis. In order that cost comparisons can be made between the various types of condominiums, a sample purchase price of $35,000 will be used in all calculations.

All figures in the following analysis are only estimates and in no way should be construed as fact. The financing terms, although selected as typical, would have to be determined for each individual purchase, due to the fact that rates and terms fluctuate daily within the financial marketplace. It should be noted that although most condominium developments offer sources for permanent financing, this is not to say that one may not use his own banking sources if he wishes. But it must be understood that much research into the development will be required on the bank's part, and consequently a single mortgage may not justify such review. Although the following analyses assume that the purchaser wishes to minimize his cash payment, one may, of course, pay for his unit in total so as to minimize his monthly expenses and eliminate interest costs.

The financial obligations of the residential condominiums are much like those of the single family home and are treated first. The finances of the resort condominium are analyzed next and are somewhat more complex due to the potential income derived from rentals and the added tax shelter savings from expense deductions and depreciation. Lastly, the finances of the commercial condominium are reviewed.

Financing a Residential Condominium

Residential condominium ownership offers the same benefits as offered under single family ownership. And such ownership is available at prices that are generally 10% to 30% less than comparable single family homes. But this price difference can be considerably less if there are common condominium recreational facilities available, as discussed in the previous section, Analyzing the Condominium Marketplace.

It should be pointed out that the main objective of this section is not to compare single family homes versus condominiums, but to show how one should analyze a typical residential condominium cost sheet. The obligations of single family home ownership are used mainly as a point of reference. To compare the advantages and disadvantages of the two forms of ownership, one should refer to the section, Why Buy a Residential Condominium?

First, a general description of financing a residential condominium is presented, which is followed by a more detailed financing description. Both descriptions refer to the cost figures generated on the sample $35,000 residential condominium cost sheet on page 84. It is very important that the cost sheets be continually referred to for a clearer understanding of the financial picture. Lastly, the residential condominium cost sheet is analyzed from the purchaser's viewpoint.

A general description of financing a residential condominium

The financial responsibilities of owning a residential condominium are very similar to the general ownership responsibilities previously discussed for the single family home. The condominium unit is individually financed as if it were a single family home, is assessed individually for real estate taxes as if it were a single family home, and is charged a monthly maintenance fee. These three cost categories are shown on the sample cost sheet on page 84 under Out-of-Pocket Costs Before Taxes.

On an after tax basis, the condominium owner has the same tax benefits as the single family home owner. He may deduct all mortgage interest and real estate taxes from his taxable income, thereby lowering his yearly taxes. Such tax savings when substracted from one's total Out-of-Pocket Costs Before Taxes equals the Effective Cost After Taxes.

The Real Cost of Ownership is computed by reducing the Effective Cost by the amortization savings, or in effect, the principal payments paid.

The Effective Cost After Resale assumes a value appreciation factor and further reduces the cost of ownership over the long run.

Such costs are further discussed in the following section.

Detailed Financing Considerations—Residential Condominiums

A more detailed description of the responsibilities and benefits of residential condominium ownership are discussed below. In order that the generation of costs and savings be fully understood, the sample $35,000 residential condominium cost sheet must be continually referred to during the reading of this section.

A typical $35,000 residential condominium might be described as follows:

> A condominium unit in a modern downtown or suburban housing complex which consists of two bedrooms, 1 bath, a combination living room-dining room, a small kitchen, and front hallway. The common facilities include a well furnished lobby, community function rooms, and adequate parking facilities.

The various ownership obligations and benefits of such a condominium are explained under the following three headings, Initial Cash Investment, Monthly Condominium Expenses, and Condominium Ownership Benefits.

Initial cash investment

The initial cash payment on a residential condominium generally ranges between 20% and 30% of the sales price of the condominium. As shown on the residential condominium cost sheet, page 84, 25% of the $35,000 condominium is required as a cash payment totaling $8,750. At the time of purchase, all legal documents would be recorded and passed, lawyer's fees would be paid, and the cash payment of $8,750 would be made, less any deposit previously paid to reserve the unit (usually 10% of the purchase).

Monthly condominium expenses

Upon passing purchase papers, one assumes a monthly cost obligation, termed Out-of-Pocket Costs Before Taxes, which includes the Mortgage Obligation, the Real Estate Taxes, and the Maintenance Fee.

Mortgage obligation

The mortgage obligation for the residential condominium is identical to the obligation for the single family home. Such a mortgage obligation generally varies between 70% and 80% of the sales price of the condominium unit with interest rates between 7% and 8%, and payback periods between 20 and 30 years.

In the example shown, a 75% mortgage obligation is chosen as typical at a 7½% rate over a 25 year period. The principal and interest payments are averaged over a ten-year period* and amount to $532.00 for the principal payments per year and $1,796.00 for the interest payments per year.

Real estate taxes

The real estate tax is the next category which is paid most often on a monthly basis to the bank holding the mortgage. The bank, in turn, pays the city on a yearly basis. As in the case of single family homes, condominium units are assessed individually for real estate taxes. Unless the local board of assessors indicates a reduced assessment value for condominiums, it must be assumed that condominium units are assessed and taxed on the same basis as single family homes. The system most commonly used to determine the tax figure is to multiply the city's tax rate per $1,000 of assessed value times the assessed value of the unit. The sales price of the unit is often used as the basis for assessment. In the example being discussed, an assessment system of 70% times the condominium sales price might be used, which is slightly lower than the 75% assessment system that was used for a single family home in the previous section.

*Explained in previous section, page 67

The yearly tax charge for the $35,000 condominium would therefore equal 70% × $35,000 × tax rate per $1,000 of assessed value, or $1,300 per year, assuming the same tax rate is used as in the case of the single family home, $53 per $1,000 of assessed value.

When purchasing any condominium, make certain that the local assessors have been consulted and that the figures presented in the offering plan are realistic. By knowing the local city's assessment technique, the local tax rate per $1,000 of project value, and the trend of tax increases, one can easily check the authenticity of any tax figures presented.

Maintenance fee

The maintenance fee is the third category which is paid on a monthly basis to the association of condominium owners. Such fees, in conjunction with the fees of other units, cover all management services as previously discussed in the management section. An estimated figure of $900 per year is shown, as actual fees are slightly less than those for single family homes, due to the shared nature of such services. And one has the added advantage of not being personally involved in such upkeep chores. The only disadvantage contemplated under condominium ownership is that the condominium maintenance fee is fixed, which limits the condominium owner from lowering costs of maintenance during times of tight money. This, of course, is not the case under single family home ownership where the home owner can somewhat lower the cost requirements as he sees fit by deferring some less urgent maintenance work, or by doing work himself which he might otherwise leave out.

The condominium monthly maintenance fee is determined by one's percentage ownership in the building as calculated by the following formula:

$$\text{Condominium Unit Maintenance Fee} = \text{Monthly Building Maintenance Budget} \times \text{Unit Ownership Percentage}$$

The total monthly expenses of condominium ownership including the mortgage payment, the real estate taxes, and the maintenance fee, as shown on the sample cost sheet, totals $377.32 for the $35,000 condominium. These figures, although significantly more stable than rental figures, can fluctuate from year to year due to tax increases or changes in maintenance costs.

Condominium ownership benefits

The ownership benefits offered to the condominium owner are very much similar to the benefits offered to the single family home owner. Such benefits which include tax savings, equity growth, and value appreciation are discussed next.

Tax benefits

Because the tax savings available to condominium owners are identical to those available to single family home owners, all mortgage interest payments and property taxes are deductible from the condominium owner's taxable income. In the residential condominium example shown on page 84, the total deductions amount to $3,096.00, which, when deducted from one's taxable income, produces a substantial tax savings. Such a tax savings can be approximated by multiplying one's tax bracket times the total deductions. (35% bracket × $3,096.00 = $1,083.60/year).

Equity growth

Condominium owners, like single family home owners, also benefit from equity growth through monthly principal payments, which effectively reduce the balance of the mortgage loan. Such payments should be viewed as an investment in one's condominium rather than a cost. In the example shown, the principal payment of $532/year when subtracted from the Effective Cost After Taxes produces a Real Cost of Ownership of $2,912.40 per year, or $242.69/month.

Value appreciation

The last consideration shown on most condominium cost sheets is the potential value appreciation due to inflation. In this example, assuming a 3% rate increase per year, the particular property has the potential to increase in value by approximately $1,050.00 per year, or 3% × $35,000. If the condominium was sold after a certain period of time and such value appreciation did take place, the Actual Cost of owning that condominium after resale would have been $1,862 per year or effectively $155.19 per month.

Analyzing the Cost Sheet

In order to reach a final purchasing decision, one must be confident that the costs projected on an offering's cost sheet are realistic and are appropriate for one's individual case. It is therefore most important that the cost data be further questioned, and the effective costs be recalculated with the individual's tax bracket, mortgage terms, etc.. Upon completion of such analysis, one can more easily reach a purchasing decision, as all costs will be specified and understood.

Questioning the cost sheet data

The first step in any financial analysis is to question the validity of the cost data. The following types of questions should help in such verification:

1) Is mortgage financing being made available? By whom?
2) Has the lending institution agreed to the mortgage terms as detailed in the cost sheet?
3) Have the projected maintenance costs been broken down by service category and verified by a qualified professional management company?
4) How have the yearly real estate taxes been calculated? Have they been verified by the local board of assessors? Remember: Property Taxes = Assessment Value of the Condominium Unit × Local Tax Rate.
5) Have the principal and interest mortgage payments been averaged over a ten-year period so as to project a realistic interest deduction amount?
   If the principal and interest payments have not been averaged over a reasonable time period, and the first year's interest payment is used for the deduction amount, an unrealistic tax savings picture will be presented due to the fact that the interest payments are more heavily weighted in the first few years of the mortgage.
6) What tax bracket level has the developer used in his cost calculations to arrive at a tax savings amount? Is it appropriate? If not, recalculate the savings using the correct bracket. Remember to use the tax bracket that is appropriate for

one's adjusted level of taxable income, not one's gross level of income.

7) Can the appreciation rate percentage presented be verified by condominium resales in the area?

How realistic are the effective costs?

After verifying the project cost figures, one should then reanalyze the effective costs after taxes. The residential condominium cost sheet on page 84 is used as reference for such an analysis.

First of all, one must realize that no matter what the effective costs are after federal tax savings, one is obligated to pay the monthly out of pocket costs during the year. Consequently, in the example shown, $377.32 is required monthly, and only when tax statements are filed after the year is out, will some of the cost be refunded through tax savings.

From an effective cost viewpoint, the only realistic effective cost calculation from a yearly cash flow consideration is the Effective Cost After Taxes. The equity and appreciation factors become effective only after the condominium is sold, and have little to do with the yearly cost of carrying the condominium. The effective cost after taxes for the sample $35,000 condominium amounts to $287.02 per year. But such an effective cost does not show the possible bank interest lost due to the initial cash payment of $8,750. Such a down payment obviously changes one's monetary situation, as such, the interest on the $8,750 is no longer accumulating cash in his bank account. Taking such a loss into consideration, the Effective Cost of Ownership After Taxes might be more realistically projected as follows:

82

Effective Cost of Ownership After Taxes

		Yearly	Monthly
Out-of-Pocket Costs		$4,528.00	$377.32
Less: Tax Savings	$1,083.00		
Plus: Interest Lost (5%)*	284.34		
Total Savings		799.26	66.60
Effective Cost After Taxes		$3,728.74	$310.72

*Interest lost after taxes on $8,750 at 5% interest rate. Assumes a 35% Tax Bracket.

Most important of all the effective cost considerations is the tax savings calculation. Is the tax bracket shown appropriate for the prospective purchaser? If not, the correct tax bracket must be inserted and the effective costs recalculated.

In order to show more clearly what effect different tax brackets have on various priced condominiums, the following chart has been formulated. Still assumed is 75% mortgage financing at a 7½% interest rate over 25 years. The out-of-pocket costs are typical for the various priced condominiums.

Condominium Purchase Price	Out-of-Pocket Costs/Month	Effective Cost/Month (Includes Tax Savings & Equity Growth)		
		20% Bracket	35% Bracket	50% Bracket
$20,000	$200–$240	$150–$170	$130–$150	$100–$120
$35,000	$350–$400	$260–$300	$220–$260	$185–$225
$50,000	$520–$570	$380–$420	$330–$350	$270–$310

Residential Condominium Cost Sheet
Sales Price $35,000
Cash Required (25%) $8,750
Mortgage (75%) $26,250
Terms 7½/25 yrs

	Yearly	Monthly
Out-of-Pocket Costs Before Taxes		
Mortgage Principal Payment	$ 532.00	$ 44.33
(10 year average)		
Mortgage Interest Payment	1,796.00	149.66
(10 year average)		
Real Estate Taxes	1,300.00	108.33
Maintenance Fee	900.00	75.00
Total Out-of-Pocket Costs	$4,528.00	$377.32
Effective Costs After Taxes		
Out-of-Pocket Costs	$4,528.00	$377.32
Less:		
Tax Savings from Deductions		
Deductions available:		
Mortgage Interest $1,796.00		
Real Estate Taxes 1,300.00		
Total Deductions $3,096.00		
Tax Savings (35% Tax Bracket)	1,083.60	90.30
Effective Cost After Taxes	$3,444.40	$287.02
Less:		
Amortization Savings (Equity Growth)	532.00	44.33
Real Cost of Ownership	$2,912.40	$242.69
Less:		
Appreciation in Value (3%/year)	1,050.00	87.50
Actual Cost After Resale	$1,862.40	$155.19

Financing a Resort Condominium

The purchase of a resort condominium can be a very enjoyable and profitable investment. But it can also be a very aggravating and costly venture if the offering is not properly analyzed prior to purchase. It is therefore the objective of this section to review all the facets of resort condominium ownership so that such costly experiences can be avoided.

The financial responsibilities of resort condominium ownership are generally more complex than the responsibilities of residential condominium ownership due to the income derived from rentals. Such rental income helps to offset expenses and consequently offers the potential of a fine investment. Because the financial responsibilities of a non rental resort condominium are no different than those of a residential condominium, the following section covers only *rental* resort condominiums.

First, a general description of financing a year around rental resort condominium is presented, and is followed by a more detailed discussion of the various financial considerations. Next to be presented is a discussion on the costs involved in taking a vacation at one's rental resort condominium. A third discussion describes the financing implicatons of part-time rental condominiums. The financial section then presents a method to help analyze the cost data and cash flow projections. Finally, the rental resort condominium is analyzed from an investment viewpoint.

A General Description of Financing a Rental Resort Condominium

The financing of a rental resort condominium can be best described through the use of a sample condominium offering.

Such an offering is displayed in the form of a cost sheet on page 110, which is to be used as reference material for the following discussion. It will be assumed in this discussion that the resort condominium is available for rent *year round,* as such assumptions are often made in actual sales literature. A more realistic approach will be analyzed later which assumes a part-time rental situation.

The typical resort condominium to be discussed costs $35,-000 as shown on the cost sheet on page 110. Initially, a certain percentage of the sales price is required as a cash payment as well as an additional cash payment for furnishings. The purchase of such furnishings is a requirement in most rental resort condominium offerings so as to standardize the units for purposes of rental. If such a stipulation is not required, the prospective purchaser should question the validity of the rental program.

The yearly projected costs are shown before and then after taxes on the cost sheet. Included in the cash flow before taxes are the Rental Income, the Ownership Expenses, and Rental Expenses. The Rental Income less the Ownership and Rental Expenses results in a cash flow per month which may be either positive or negative. A negative cash flow, as shown, is not uncommon due to the seasonal nature of most rental programs. But such a negative cash flow can be offset by tax savings, equity growth and appreciation as discussed in the following sections.

The rental income of a resort condominium is subject to taxation as in any rental property. But, if one's tax deductible expenses exceed such a rental income, one is granted a tax savings. Such tax savings can be approximated by multiplying one's proper tax bracket percentage times the difference between the total deductible expenses and the rental income. Such computations can be better visualized by referring to the sample cost sheet on page 110. The allowable deductions include three of the four Ownership Expenses (mortgage interest, maintenance fees, real estate taxes), Rental Expenses and Depreciation. The Net Cost After Taxes can therefore be determined by subtracting the tax savings from the cash flow figure before taxes. The resulting net cost can be either positive or negative which depends mainly on the rental income and one's tax bracket.

Detailed Financing Considerations—Rental Condominium

The responsibilities and benefits of owning year-round rental resort condominium are discussed in further detail in this section. The sample offering described in the previous section and shown on page 110 will be the basis for the discussion. It will be assumed that the condominium being offered is rented year around and is described as follows:

> The condominium unit is in a contemporary modular housing cluster located on a mountainside overlooking a winter ski resort area. The unit includes two bedrooms (one in the loft), 1 bathroom, a combination living and dining area, kitchen, and sundeck. The area offers skiing in the winter and golf, swimming and tennis in the summer. Common facilities include saunas, tennis courts, and game room.

The responsibilities and benefits of owning such a condominium are explained under the following three headings: Initial Cash Investment, Yearly Income and Expenses, and Benefits of a Resort Condominium.

87

Initial cash investment

The initial cash payment on a resort condominium generally ranges between 20% and 30% of the sales price of the condominium, very much like that of the residential condominium. In the example shown, 25% of the $35,000 condominium is required equaling $8,750. Also required in most rental resort condominiums is the requirement to purchase furnishings which may vary from $3,000 to $8,000. Shown in the example is a $5,000 requirement for such furnishings, which in combination with the down payment equals a total initial cash outlay of $13,750. Such an initial cash payment can be reduced by financing the furnishings over a short period of time (2 to 8 years). But in order to not over-complicate the sample cost sheet, it will be assumed in the example that the total furnishing package is purchased outright.

Yearly income and expenses (cash flow)

The cash flow of a rental resort condominium takes into account the Rental Income, the Ownership Expenses, and the Rental Expenses, all of which are described below.

Rental income

The Rental Income of a resort condominium helps to offset Ownership expenses, as well as the resulting Rental Expenses. Projections of Rental Income are usually based on past rental performance but in the case of new offerings which have never been rented, projections are often estimated. Such estimates are based on weekly or daily occupancy projections. In the sample offering described, the projections assumed a 60% occupancy in the winter on a weekly basis and a 40% occupancy in the summer months, also on a weekly basis. Obviously in this example the rental income during the winter season is more favorable due to the availability of skiing. Also shown is a daily occupancy projection of 21 days during the off season of fall and spring. The total income projected for the sample resort condominium at the weekly rates shown amounts to $4,060.00/year.

Ownership expenses

The Monthly Ownership Expenses include the *mortgage obligation,* the *real estate taxes,* and the *maintenance fees.* The mortgage obligation, for a resort condominium, generally varies between 65% and 85% of the sales price of the condominium at an interest rate between 7% and 9%. It should be noted that interest rates on second homes are slightly higher than those on first homes, depending on the area of the country. In the example shown, a 75% mortgage commitment will be assumed at a 7½% rate over a 25 year period. The principal and interest payments per year, averaged over the first ten years of the mortgage, total $2,328/year ($532 + $1,796).

The maintenance fee has been estimated at $600 per year which is $300 less than required by the residential condominium example due to the absence of heat and utility payments, and in most cases, hallway cleaning services. In resort condominiums, such heat and utility charges are most often budgeted under Rental Operating Expenses (described later), and often hallway cleaning services are eliminated due to the use of private entranceways in low-rise structures. The $600 fee does continue to cover such areas as exterior ground maintenance, snow removal, exterior painting and repairs, gardening, recreational facility upkeep, reserve fund for contingencies, and insurance.

The real estate tax which is considerably less than the residential condominium property tax, due to the lower tax rates in resort areas, is estimated for the above example at $500 per year. Local tax assessors should be consulted for confirmation of such rates.

The total ownership costs for the example shown equals $3,428.00/year or $284.83/month, which includes the mortgage payment, the maintenance fee and the real estate taxes.

Rental expenses

The second main category of expenses is the Rental Expenses which includes a *rental management fee, laundry and maid service,* and *operating expenses.* The rental management and cleaning fees are directly related to the volume of rental business and are therefore often calculated as a percentage of the total income. In the example shown, 15% of the rental income has been estimated for both the rental and cleaning services, as such fees vary between 10% and 20% of the rental income.

The operating expenses are estimated at $550 which cover all heat and utility services for the unit, as well as any unit repairs, assuming a rental activity level of $4,060. This, of course, also varies with the volume of rental business, but is generally not shown as a percentage of rental income.

The total rental management costs for the example shown equal $1,770.00 per year or $147.50 per month.

The Cash Flow Before Taxes is determined by taking the difference between the Rental Income and the total of the Ownership expense plus Rental Expenses. In the example shown, the expenses exceed the rental income by $1,138/year or $147.50/month.

Benefits of owning a resort condominium

The benefits of owning a rental producing resort condominium are many, for not only does one receive a substantial tax shelter, but also receives equity growth through the principal payments and a potential value appreciation of his unit through inflation.

Tax shelter

Due to the income nature of the resort condominium, one must pay taxes on all profits generated during the year, and conversely may claim tax savings on any losses. To determine whether one has a savings or a loss, one must compare the Deductible Expenses against the Rental Income. If the Deductible Expenses exceed the rental income, tax savings are generated as shown in the example. The tax savings are approximated by multiplying one's tax bracket times one's net deductible expenses, as previously indicated in the residential condominium analysis. Under the resort condominium, the Net Deductible Expense is determined by subtracting the Rental Income from the total deductible expenses.

Almost all expenses are deductible from taxable income under rental condominium property. Mortgage Interest and Real Estate Taxes are deductible, as is the case for the residential condominium. But unlike a residential condominium, Maintenance Fees (part of Ownership Expenses) and Rental Expenses are deductible due to the business status of the property; and all furniture and buildings may be depreciated. In the example shown, the sum of the deductible expenses, $6,870.00, less the Rental Income, $4,060.00, leaves a Net Deductible Expense of $2,810.00 per year. The depreciation figures are explained in Appendix E. Assuming a tax bracket of 35% the approximate tax savings are calculated by multiplying 35% times the net deductible figure of $2,810.00 which equals a $984.00 tax savings. Such a savings, when added to the cash flow figure before taxes results in a Net Cost after Taxes of $154.00.

The resort condominium illustrated is therefore almost self-supporting, for in effect, most of the yearly expenses are paid by rental income and tax savings.

Equity growth

An important consideration in any purchase is the building of equity growth, for even if the rental resort condominium costs a small amount of money each year, a good percentage of equity is being built up. In the above example, the principal payment which goes toward equity growth, amounts to $532 per year over an average of 10 years.

Value appreciation

Due to the close proximity to recreational areas, most resort condominiums appreciate in value at a substantial rate per year. An appreciation rate of 5% per year is not uncommon and can amount to as much as $17,500 over a 10-year period. It is therefore important to check the rates of appreciation of similar units in the area.

One often hears such statements as "enjoy cost-free vacations in your own rental resort condominium." This statement is somewhat misleading as such vacations can significantly reduce the rental income produced by one's unit. Because owners of rental resort condominiums often enjoy their premises during vacation periods, it is important that one understands the implications of a "cost-free vacation."

Let us assume, for example, that the owner of a $35,000 winter year around rental resort condominium described in the previous section, decides to use his condominium for two weeks during the ski season and one week during the summer season. Because the condominium will not be rentable during those weeks, the rental income from the unit will be lowered. Such a loss of income is approximated on the cost sheet on page 112. As shown by the cost sheet, the rental income is reduced from $4,060 to $3,528, or by $532.

Such a rental reduction would have the following effect on the cash flow as indicated on the cost sheet on page 112. Refer to this cost sheet when considering the following information.

Considering the cash flow before taxes first, it quickly becomes apparent that although the Ownership Expenses remain the same, the Rental Expenses are somewhat reduced. This is due to the fact that the rental management fee and laundry services are determined on a percentage of Rental Income which is lower. The operating expenses would remain the same, due to the continued use of the facilities, by the owner rather than the renter.

Therefore, the total expenses would be slightly less than if renting year around. But because the Rental Income is significantly less, the negative cash drain has increased by $368.00 to $1,506.00 per year before taxes. It immediately becomes quite evident the three-week vacation at one's own condominium is not exactly free. The net cost after taxes is described below, and although some of the vacation's cost is reduced through greater tax savings, the reduction is not significant enough to justify the statement "Enjoy cost-free vacations in your own resort condominium."

The tax savings calculations are of course also slightly different due to the change in the rental period. It is important to understand that one may deduct Maintenance and Rental Expenses only over the period of *rental* availability. Such is also the case with depreciation. Therefore in the above example, the Maintenance and Rental Expenses are deductible only over 49 of the 52 weeks of the year. The remaining three weeks are unavailable for rental, and therefore only mortgage interest and real estate tax deductions can be taken. The overall effect of such a rental period change is as follows:

The Maintenance Fee is deductible over only 49 weeks of the year, therefore 49/52 of the $600 fee, or $564, is deductible. In the case of the Rental Expenses, the rental management fee and the laundry services have already been reduced due to their percentage relationship with the Rental Income, which is lower. But the third category of Rental Expenses, that being operating expenses, would be deductible only over the 49-week period, much like that of the Maintenance Fee. Therefore the deductible operating expenses would be reduced to $519 from $550, causing the deductible rental expenses to be reduced to $1,575 from $1,770. As indicated briefly above, the building and furniture are also only depreciable over the rental period. Therefore, 49/52 of the depreciable amount may be deducted.

Consequently the deductible expense totals $6,513 instead of the previous $6,870. But the Net Deductible Expenses are increased due to the lower rental income figure, which offers a slight tax savings on the increased cash flow before taxes. Such tax savings amount to $1,041.00 per year as compared to $984.00 for the previous example, again assuming a 35% tax bracket. The tax savings, when added to the cash flow before taxes, nets a cost per year of $465.00 as compared to $154.00 for the previous example.

It is therefore concluded that the three-week vacation is in reality not free but costs the owner $311, which is the cash flow difference between the two examples displayed. Such calculations should always be made when considering a vacation at one's year-around rental condominium, for most cost sheets disregard the impact of one's vacation.

Although it is obvious that such vacations at one's own condominium are not free, the cost is minimal, when compared to the cost of renting elsewhere. For example, if one was to rent someone else's condominium for the prices indicated in the previous example, he would pay $980 (two weeks × $350/week plus one week × $280/wk). Although one might argue that by renting someone else's condominium, at least one does not lose his own rentals, the argument is unjustified for the $311 gained from not vacationing in one's own condominium does not offset the $980 cost of vacationing somewhere else. Therefore enjoy your own condominium during vacations at a slight cost.

Financing a Part-Time Rental Resort Condominium

The prospective condominium buyer who plans to purchase a resort condominium so that he may rent it out part-time and use it for his own use part-time should become fully aware of the Internal Revenue Service's newest regulation on part-time rental condominiums. As of July, 1972, the Internal Revenue Service has tightened the tax benefits for owners renting out their vacation home or condominium on a part-time basis. Basically, the regulation states that if the condominium rentals are not considered to be an activity "engaged in for profit," one's aggregate deductions on the condominium can not exceed one's gross rental income from the activity. Such a ruling does not affect the investor who buys a condominium unit with the sole objective of renting it out year-round for investment purposes, even if the aggregate deductions exceed the income from the property. It also does not restrict any condominium owner from declaring basic ownership deductions such as the mortgage interest and the real estate taxes.

To best show the impact of the above regulations on owners who rent out their condominium on a part-time basis, a sample condominium cost sheet is shown on page 114 which compares the tax savings under both the new and old tax regulations. Shown is a $35,000 summer resort condominium which is usable four months a year during the resort season. During two months of the season, the condominium is rented out at $1,250 per month, and for the other two months, the owner uses the condominium himself. This results in a $2,500 income per year which helps to offset the ownership expenses before taxes, which include the mortgage payments, the maintenance fee, the utility payments, and the real estate taxes. Because the rental program is not considered to be an activity "engaged in for profit," the tax regulation change affects the amount of deductions that can be taken. In any case, one can always take the mortgage interest and real estate taxes as a tax deduction. Under the old regulations, one could also deduct depreciation, all maintenance expenses, and utility expenses that were accountable to the rental period. In the example shown, since the rental period took up one-half of the rental season, one-half of the total expenses plus depreciation could be deducted. When such deductible expenses amounted to more than the rental income, a tax savings occurred as shown in the example, page 114.

Under the new regulations such deductible expenses can not exceed the rental income in a non-profit part-time rental activity. Therefore, it can be seen by the example, a limit of $2,500 is placed upon the deductible expenses resulting in no tax savings. Only for the case where the mortgage interest and real estate taxes exceed the rental income would one receive a tax savings. For instance, if the rental income was $2,000 instead of $2,500, the mortgage interest and real estate taxes alone would exceed the rental income, $2,296 versus $2,000. Therefore, even in the part-time rental situation, one would gain a tax savings from a net deductible expense of $296. In the example shown on page 114, the rental income exceeded the mortgage interest and real estate taxes by $204. Therefore one may allocate a portion of the rental period's maintenance expenses, utility expenses, and depreciation to make up the $204 difference.

The cash loss resulting from the regulation change can be considerable depending on one's tax bracket. For the example shown, a $472 difference is noted. But one should not forget that the rental income even under the new regulations helps considerably to lower expenses before and after taxes.

Although the new tax regulations will require prospective resort condominium buyers to be more cautious when purchasing condominiums to be rented out part-time, there are new approaches to tax savings which should be considered. For example, one might purchase a resort condominium without a mortgage by increasing the mortgage amount on his city home. This, in effect, would apply the previous condominium mortage interest to the city house, and as a result, would allow the other expenses plus the real estate taxes to offset the rental income. Another possible approach to tax savings would be to consider a separate lease for the use of one's personal property, i.e., furniture, snowmobile, boat, etc. Since there would be little mortgage interest and no real estate taxes on such items, one would not be prevented from taking the appropriate depreciation and maintenance deductions on the personal property, thereby better utilizing such deductions.

It is most important that one understand that, in many situations, it is difficult to determine which tax regulation is most appropriate for the rental situation. If the purchase of a condominium hinges on the answer to such a question, it is imperative that one consult his tax accountant or the Internal Revenue Service before purchasing.

Analyzing the Condominium Offering

In order to reach a purchase decision, more information is required than has been shown in the previous sections. It is therefore the purpose of this section to familiarize the potential buyer with the types of questions that must be asked, and the types of areas which should be further explained. First of all, the offering plan data must be questioned and verified. Then, the cash flow projections must be further analyzed both from a monthly and yearly basis. Both areas are discussed below.

Questioning the offering plan data

The data presented in any resort condominium offering plan must be checked for its authenticity. Such an analysis can be best carried out through a series of questions much like those as presented in the residential condominium section. But further questions are required for a resort condominium, as it has the added dimension of being an income-making property. Therefore, in addition to the residential condominium questions, one must ask the following questions which relate specifically to a rental resort condominium:

1) Is one required to join the rental pool?
2) If one does join the rental pool are there restrictions as to when the owner can use the condominium? How much notice is required to reserve the condominium for one's own use?
3) Have the rental projections been based on activity levels from previous years' operations? If not, who is to say that they are realistic?
4) Have similar rentals in the area been checked for occupancy percentages and rate schedules to check the authenticity of the rental projections?
5) What organization will have the responsibility for promoting and managing the rental pool business? What experience has the management organization had in such rental programs?
6) Has the rental management service been defined so as to include advertising budgets, promotion programs, and rental outlets? These are usually important to help maintain the projected rental income.
7) Have the laundry and maid services been adequately budgeted? In other words, have all the services been broken

down and individually costed—labor costs, cleaning cost, etc.?

8) On what basis has the building and furniture been depreciated? Straight line, 150% declining balance, 200% declining balance, etc. (Check the depreciation description in Appendix E to verify such calculations.)

9) Is it clear that the rental program will be reviewed as an activity "engaged in for profit" so that full tax savings can be taken?

How realistic are the cash flow projections?

In order to protect one's self from unexpected costs, the condominium cost sheet must be further analyzed from a cash flow basis. Such cash flows are analyzed first on a yearly basis and secondly on a monthly basis. The cost sheet on page 110 will be used as reference.

Cash flow on a yearly basis

The cost of financing a resort condominium varies considerably depending on the rental income amount and the individual owner's tax bracket level. It is therefore imperative that the rental income projections be well justified on past year's operations, or be forecasted by professional estimators. Because the projections of most offerings tend to be overly optimistic, it is important that the purchaser analyze the offering at various levels of yearly rental income to determine the effect on yearly costs before and after taxes. In the table shown below, four levels of rental income have been analyzed for the $35,000 resort condominium previously presented. Three different tax bracket levels have also been used to show their effect on the different owner's yearly costs.

100

Cash Flow at Various Levels of Rental Income
Brackets ( ) indicate a negative cash loss

Rental Income/Yr.	Cash Flow Before Taxes	Cash Gain (Loss) After Taxes		
		20% Tax B	35% Tax B	50% Tax B
$6,000	$ 172	$ 472	$697	$992
5,000	(503)	(68)	258	585
4,060	(1,138)	(576)	(154)	267
3,000	(1,728)	(1,048)	(538)	(28)
2,000	(2,328)	(1,518)	(910)	(303)

The table shown above confirms the inevitable relationship between rental income and costs before taxes; as rentals decrease, yearly costs increase. Such yearly costs can be significant as shown by the $2,000 rental income level. But what is more interesting to note is that the variation in costs after taxes is much less significant especially at higher tax levels. Because the tax bracket level does have such an influence on the cash requirements after taxes, it is important to use one's own tax bracket level in such calculations.

Such an exercise can be invaluable to the purchaser who is overly concerned about the projected rental income estimate and needs to know what effect a lower rental income will have on the yearly costs.

Cash flow on a monthly basis

The monthly carrying costs before taxes are generally not shown on rental resort condominium cost sheets, but are often approximated by dividing the yearly costs by 12 months. But this is sometimes misleading, for one must remember that the rental income stream is quite variable depending on the season, and consequently, during the off seasons, the monthly carrying costs may be considerably higher than the carrying cost averaged over the year. Therefore one must be prepared to carry the total cost of the expenses during the off season months.

It is also important for one to question the procedure of reimbursement for rental in :ome. One may find that rental income cannot be reimbursed to the owner by the rental management company for a period of one to two months after such income has been received due to the system of accounting used by that company. Such details should be well defined before any decision of purchase is made.

Analyzing the Rental Resort Condominium as an Investment

It is important that all rental resort condominiums being purchased for investment purposes be well justified through some type of financial analysis. Although there are different methods of analysis, the individual methods each address a different investment viewpoint. For instance, if one were interested in investing in a rental resort condominium for a yearly cash return on his initial investment, a *Return on Investment Analysis* would be recommended. If the reason for investment was for a future one time cash gain, a *Capital Gains Analysis* would be recommended. (See page 105.) A third type of analysis might be a *Long Term Growth Analysis* which determines whether or not one should purchase now for retirement purposes later. (See pg. 108.)

The following section illustrates the use of these three methods of analysis through the use of the cost data presented in the rental resort condominium shown on pg. 111. It is important to note that no matter how sophisticated the analysis, the conclusion invariably depends on how fast one expects the value of the condominium to appreciate, and what level of rental income is expected. It is for this reason that the following illustrations take into consideration various rental income levels and various value appreciation rates.

Return on investment

The Return on Investment Analysis is performed so as to determine the percentage rate of return that one can expect from an initial cash investment in a rental resort condominium. The percentage rate of return can then be compared with simple savings bank rates to determine whether the purchase of the condominium is an advantageous investment.

Shown below is a return on investment analysis for the $35,000 rental resort condominium previously discussed, page 110. The initial cash investment required is $13,750, which includes both the cash payment and the furnishings. The question to be answered is whether such an investment will return a satisfactory percentage income return per year. Such a return on investment is calculated by the following formula:

% Return on Investment = $\dfrac{\text{Cash Gain (Loss) After Taxes}}{\text{Initial Cash Investment}}$
(After Taxes)

The return on investment is calculated on an after tax basis due to the fact that rental resort condominiums offer significant tax savings. On a before tax basis, the cash flow for most resort condominiums is minimal if not negative and is obviously not competitive with other alternatives of investment.

Using the cost and cash flow figures from the previous resort condominium example shown on page 110 the following rates of return can be calculated assuming a 35% tax bracket.

103

Rental Income/Yr.	Cash Gain (Loss)* After Taxes (35% tax bracket)	% Return on Investment (After Taxes)
$6,000	$697	5.1%
$5,000	$258	1.9%
$4,060	($154)	(1.1%)

In order to compare such rates of return for the various levels of rental income with savings banks' rates, one must convert the bank rates to an after tax basis. Consequently, assuming a 35% tax bracket, a 5% bank interest rate before taxes amounts to approximately a 3.25% interest rate after taxes. (.65 × .05)

When comparing this 3.25% interest rate with the condominium percentage returns, it becomes obvious that the percent return on investment for the resort condominium assuming $6,000 rental income level is truly superior to the savings' bank return (5.1% versus 3.25% after taxes). But when considering a more realistic rental income level, like $4,060 per year, the condominium investment rate of return no longer exceeds the savings banks' rates; in fact, the rate shown above for the $4,060 rental income level is negative, which indicates a cash loss after taxes. The influence of the rental income level becomes quite evident. Although a higher tax bracket level and/or a lower initial cash investment through furniture financing would somewhat increase the rate of return, the cash gains would still not be competitive with alternate investments.

It can therefore be concluded that in most cases, one will find it difficult to justify an investment in a rental resort condominium strictly on a cash rate of return. But when analyzed on a long term basis with the consideration of such factors as equity growth and value appreciation, the investment appears

*Shown on cash flow table, page 101.

much more favorable. Such factors are taken into consideration in the following two analyses.

Capital gains investment

The investment in a resort condominium is often analyzed from a capital gains viewpoint. Basically, the analysis determines the net cash gain that one can expect from purchasing a rental resort condominium today and selling it after a certain period of time. Such a capital gain can be then compared against gains from other investment alternatives to determine which investment should be undertaken.

Because such an analysis depends so heavily on the future sales price of the condominium, it is imperative that various rates of value appreciation be considered. The following chart projects potential future sales value for the sample $35,000 condominium over a 20-year period at both a 3% and 5% rate of value appreciation.

Future Sales Value

Ownership Period	0	5	10	15	20
Sales Value (3% Appreciation Rate/Yr.)	$35,000	$40,500	$46,800	$54,400	$63,000
Appreciation Factor	1	1.16	1.34	1.56	1.80
Sales Value (5% Appreciation Rate/Yr.)	$35,000	$44,680	$57,000	$72,760	$92,820
Appreciation Factor	1	1.27	1.63	2.08	2.65

Using the sales figures above, the purchase of the $35,000 rental resort condominium is analyzed below from a capital gains viewpoint. A 10-year ownership period will be assumed, whereupon the condominium will be sold at the fair market

105

sales price. Shown below are potential sales prices of the condominium after the 10-year period, and the costs involved in purchasing and carrying the condominium over the 10-year period. The difference between the sales price and the total costs indicates the capital gain or (loss).

| | Value Appreciation Rate | |
	3%	5%
Condominium Sales Value in 10 years	$46,800*	$57,000*
Costs to Carry the Condominium over a 10 year period:		
Initial Cash Payment to Purchase	13,750	13,750
Cost to Carry Condominium 10 years**	1,540	1,540
Cost to sell Condominium thru broker (6% of Sales Price)	2,800	3,420
Balance of the loan yet to be paid (Remaining Principal)***	20,921	20,921
Total Costs	$39,011	$39,631
Net Capital Gain/Before Taxes (Assumes Sale of Condominium)	$ 7,789	$17,369
Net Capital Gain/After Taxes**** (Assumes 35% Tax Bracket)	$ 6,427	$14,319

It can be concluded from the above analysis that the purchase and sale of the sample resort condominium after 10 years of ownership offers a capital gain (cash) of $7,789 assuming a 3%

*   Derived from the Future Sales Value Table, page 105.
**   The cost to carry the condominium over the 10-year period is derived from the $35,000 resort condominium cost sheet shown on page 110 which had a cash loss after taxes of $154. Therefore, over 10 years the cost would total $1,540 (10 × $154). Example assumes that all increases in maintenance and real estate costs over the 10-year period are offset by similar increases in rental income.
***   See Loan Progress Chart pg. 62
****   Capital Gain Tax calculations are explained on pg. 108.

yearly appreciation rate and $17,369 assuming a 5% yearly appreciation rate. Such gains must be compared against alternative investment opportunities to determine their true value. When compared to the alternative of placing the initial investment of $13,750 into a savings bank at a 5% interest rate, the purchase of the condominium becomes somewhat questionable as shown below:

Cash Gain Over 10 Yr. Period

	Savings Bank Interest (5% Interest Rate)	Condominium Purchase (3% Appr)	Condominium Purchase (5% Appr)
Net Gain Before Taxes	$8,630	$7,789	$17,369
Net Gain After Taxes	$5,600	$6,427	$14,319

As seen from the above comparison, the investment decision is based mainly on which appreciation rate is used. If a 3% rate is most realistic, the net gain on a before tax basis favors the savings bank investment, although on an after tax basis, the condominium investment is favored due to the advantage of capital gains taxes (explained later in this section). If the 5% rate is more realistic, the condominium investment is truly superior. Although the condominium purchase seems more favorable overall, it must be remembered that the cost figures used in the analysis assumed a rental income per year of $4,060 which may or may not be realistic for a given condominium. The analysis also did not consider the interest lost on the $1,540 spent over the 10-year period or additional cash spent for new furnishings. On the other hand, if the furnishings were financed in the initial purchase, the initial cash investment would have

107

been lowered. This, in effect, would reduce accumulated savings in bank interest in the previous table, and therefore would enhance the condominium purchase. It is therefore most important that any offering that is analyzed from a capital gains standpoint be performed with the proper financing package, the proper rental income levels, realistic appreciation rates, proper tax brackets, correct lengths of investment, realistic depreciation, etc.

The difference in the after tax computation shown above is due to the fact that only 50% of one's capital gains are taxable whereas all the bank interest is taxable. A brief sample of the tax computations are shown below:

	Condominium Purchase (3% Appr.)	Bank interest (5%/yr. on $13,750) Over 10 years)
Net Gain Before Taxes	$7,789	$8,630
Approximate Taxable Gain	3,895	8,630
Cost of Taxes (35% Tax Bracket)	1,362	3,030
Net Gain After Taxes	$6,427	$5,600

It must be understood that such tax computations are only estimates and must be viewed as such. For further detail, a qualified tax accountant should be consulted.

Long term growth investment

A question that often arises is whether one should buy a rental resort condominium today, for retirement purposes in the future, or whether one should wait to buy the condominium upon retirement. The purpose of the following analysis is to consider such a question over a 15-year period for the $35,000 resort condominium previously discussed. In order to make the analysis truly realistic, a $3,000 rental income per year will be assumed rather than the $4,060 used previously. This assumes owner occupancy during vacations and a lesser rental activity than projected. Such a rental income requires a carrying cost of $538/year after taxes as derived in the previous section, Analyzing the Cost Sheet, page 100.

The analysis below compares the alternatives of buying the condominium today and renting it out for 15 years until retirement, against the option of waiting 15 years to buy it upon retirement. Two purchase values are shown below, one assuming a 3%/year value appreciation rate, and the second a 5% per year value appreciation rate over the 15 years.

	Value Appreciation Rates	
	3%/yr	5%/yr
Cost of Purchasing Condominium after 15 years	$54,400	$72,760
Cost to Buy Now and Carry Condominium for 15 years		
Initial Cash Payment $13,750		
Cost to Carry Condominium 15 yrs.* 8,070		
Investment in New Furnishings 6,000		
Mortgage Principle Yet to be Pd.** 16,350	44,170	44,170
Gross Dollars Saved by Purchasing Now	$10,230	$28,590
Less: Interest Lost***	9,272	9,272
Net Dollars Saved by Purchasing Now	$ 958	$19,318

---

*   Carrying costs determined by multiplying cost/year ($538) $\times$ 15 years.
**   See Loan Progress Chart pg. 62
*** Interest lost includes the interest lost on the initial cash payment of $13,750 over 15 years, the interest lost on the carrying costs of $8,070, and the interest lost on the $6,000 investment in furniture.

Resort Condominium Cost Sheet

Sales Price	$35,000
Cash Required (25%)	$ 8,750
Mortgage (75%)	$26,250
Terms-7½%/25 years	
Furniture Payment	$5,000

Projected Cash Flow

Rental Income Projections

Winter - $350/wk × 12 wks. × 60% occup.= $2,520.00
Summer - $280/wk × 10 wks. × 40% occup.=   1,120.00
Off Season Income - $20/day × 21 days =   420.00

Total Rental Income / Year		$4,060.00
Less:		
Ownership Expenses		
Mortgage Principal Payment	$ 532.00	
Mortgage Interest Payment	1,796.00	
Maintenance Fee	600.00	
Real Estate Taxes	500.00	
Total Ownership Expenses	$3,428.00	
Rental Expenses		
Rental Management Fee(15%)	$ 610.00	
Laundry and Maid Service(15%)	610.00	
Operating Expenses (Heat & Utilities)	550.00	
Total Rental Expenses	$1,770.00	
Total Expenses		5,198.00
Cash Flow Before Taxes		($1,138.00)
Add:		
Tax Benefit		
Allowable Deductions		
Mortgage Interest	$1,796.00	
Maintenance Fee	600.00	
Real Estate Taxes	500.00	
Rental Expenses	1,770.00	
Building Depreciation	1,204.00	
Furniture Depreciation	1,000.00	

Total Deductions	$6,870.00	
Less:		
Rental Income	4,060.00	
Net Deductible Exp.	$2,810.00	
Tax Savings (35% Tax Bracket)		984.00
Net Cost After Taxes		($154.00)

Resort Condominium Cost Sheet
(Includes a 3 Week Vacation)

Sales Price	$35,000	
Cash Required (25%)	$ 8,750	
Mortgage (75%)	$26,250	
Terms-7½%/25 years		
Furniture Payment	$ 5,000	

Projected Cash Flow Rental Income Projections	(Year Round Rental)	(Rental + 3 wk Vacation)
Winter-$350/wk × 10 wks × 60% occup. =		$2,100.00
Summer-$280/wk × 9 wks × 40% occup. =		1,008.00
Winter-$350/wk × 12 wks × 60% occup. =	$2,520.00	
Summer-$280/wk × 10 wks × 40% occup. =	1,120.00	
Off Season Income-$20/day × 21 days	420.00	420.00
Total Rental Income / Year	$4,060.00	$3,528.00
Less:		
Ownership Expenses		
Mortgage Principal Payment	$ 532.00	$ 532.00
Mortgage Interest Payment	1,796.00	1,796.00
Maintenance Fee	600.00	600.00
Real Estate Taxes	500.00	500.00
Total Ownership Expenses	$3,428.00	$3,428.00
Rental Expenses		
Rental Management Fee(15%)	$ 610.00	$ 528.00
Laundry & Maid Service(15%)	610.00	528.00
Operating Expenses	550.00	550.00

Total Rental Expenses	$1,770.00		$1,606.00	
Total Expenses		5,198.00		5,034.00
Cash Flow Before Taxes		($1,138.00)		($1,506.00)
Add:				
Tax Benefit				
Allowable Deductions				
Mortgage Interest	$1,796.00		$1,796.00	
Maintenance Fee	600.00		564.00	
Real Estate Taxes	500.00		500.00	
Rental Expenses	1,770.00		1,575.00	
Building Depreciation	1,204.00		1,138.00	
Furniture Depreciation	1,000.00		940.00	
Total Deductions	$6,870.00		$6,513.00	
Less:				
Rental Income	4,060.00		3,528.00	
Net Deductible Exp.	$2,810.00		$2,985.00	
Tax Savings (35% Tax Bracket)		984.00		1,041.00
Net Cost After Taxes		($ 154.00)		($ 465.00)

Part Time Rental Resort Condominium

Sales Price	$35,000
Cash Required(25%)	$ 8,750
Mortgage (75%)	$26,250
Terms-7½%–25 years	
Furniture Payment	$ 5,000

		(Old) (Regulations)	(New) (Regulations)
Projected Cash Flow			
Rental Income Projections			
Rental - 2 months at $1,250/mo		$2,500.00	$2,500.00
Less:			
Ownership Expenses			
Mortgage Principal Payment	$ 532.00		
Mortgage Interest Payment	1,796.00		
Maintenance Fee	500.00		
Utilities	400.00		
Real Estate Taxes	500.00		
Total Expenses		3,728.00	3,728.00
Cash Flow Before Taxes		($1,228.00)	($1,228.00)
Add:			
Tax Benefit			
Allowable Deductions			
Mortgage Interest	$1,796.00	$1,796.00	
Real Estate Taxes	500.00	500.00	
(Deductions Effected by Regulation Change)			
Maint. Fee ½ Actual	250.00	( )	
Utilities ½ Actual	200.00	(204.00*)	
Depreciation ½ Actual	1,102.00	( )	
Total Deductions	3,848.00	2,500.00	
Less: Rental Income	2,500.00	2,500.00	
Net Deductible Exp.	$1,348.00	0.00	
Tax Savings (35% Tax Bracket)	$ 472.00	$ 0.00	
Net Cost After Taxes	($ 756.00)	($1,228.00)	

Under the new regulation the maximum amount of deductions allowable for the maintenance fee, utilities and appreciation is the amount that the rental income exceeds the total of the mortgage interest and the real estate taxes.

On page 109 the analysis shows a favorable preference to purchasing now, especially considering the lower rental figure used and the amount of enjoyment one would gain from spending summer vacations at the resort. But it is important to remember that the $3,000 rental income level costs the owner $1,728 per year before tax savings, page 100, which may be a significant drain on one's resources. It is therefore important to consider all such factors before a purchase decision is made.

In summary, the three methods of analysis above have been presented to aid the prospective investor in analyzing actual rental condominium offerings. Because so many variables exist in any analysis, the conclusions drawn in the above examples may be entirely different than conclusions drawn from analyzing other offerings. It is therefore strongly recommended that one determine realistic yearly ownership costs before and after taxes using authentic rental income levels, and personal tax bracket levels. And then, when using such costs in the above analyses, be sure to remember to use appreciation rates that are realistic for the area being considered.

Financing a Commercial Condominium

The commercial condominium is presently becoming more and more popular in the office space marketplace. Professional individuals, as well as partnerships and corporations, are realizing for the first time that office ownership offers considerable advantages over rental. Besides the addition of an equity interest in one's own business office, the office condominium offers increased tax shelter through depreciation, and reduces the concern of spiraling rents. One also gains a voice in the building management, and enjoys the appreciation in value of the condominium real estate.

The financial responsibilities of a commercial condominium are somewhat similar to those of the year-round rental resort condominium as all yearly expenses as well as building depreciation are deductible from one's taxable income. The main difference is that there is no rental income due to the owner's use of the commercial space.

First to be presented below is a general description of the financing of a commercial condominium which is followed by a more detailed description for both individual and group ownership. The ownership offering is then further analyzed from the purchaser's viewpoint and, lastly, is compared against a similar rental offering.

A General Description of Financing a Commercial Condominium

A commercial condominium may be purchased by an individual such as an attorney, doctor, dentist, engineer, architect, or by a group such as a limited partnership or corporation.

The financial responsibilities of ownership for the individual as well as for the limited partnership or corporation are quite similar except for the slight difference in methods of taxation. Such taxation differences will be briefly discussed in the following sections.

The financing terms available for commercial condominiums are slightly more stringent than those for residential ownership due to the speculative nature of a business enterprise. Consequently, a lesser portion of the purchase price is usually financed, which in turn requires a larger initial cash payment. (25% to 40% of the purchase price). The mortgage is generally financed over a shorter period of time and at a slightly higher interest rate (7¼-9%) than shown in the previous examples. As an example of such commercial financing terms, it is recommended that the reader refer to the typical commercial condominium cost sheet as shown on page 129.

The example assumes a $35,000 commercial condominium in which 30% of the purchase price is required in cash and 70% is mortgaged over 20 years at an interest rate of 8%. For means of comparison, such terms may be compared with residential financing terms where 75% of the purchase price is usually financed over a 25-year period at a 7½% interest rate.

The Out-of-pocket Costs Before Taxes include principal and interest mortgage payments, real estate taxes, and maintenance fees, much like those of the residential condominium. But the effective cost of owning a $35,000 commercial condominium on an after tax basis is somewhat less than the cost of owning a $35,000 residential condominium due to the additional deductions allowable under business property ownership. In the example shown on page 130, the taxable income deductions allowed include mortgage interest, real estate taxes, maintenance fees, and yearly depreciation.

Such deductions offer substantial tax savings, depending primarily on one's tax bracket. Assumed in the example is an individual with a 40% tax bracket. The Effective Cost After Federal Taxes is determined by subtracting the Tax Savings figure from the Out-of-Pocket Costs Before Taxes. The Real Cost of Ownership takes amortization savings (equity growth through the principal payments) into account and therefore depicts the Real Cost of Ownership. The Actual Cost After Resale takes the potential value appreciation into account after capital gain taxes.

Financing a Commercial Condominium by an Individual

The responsibilities and benefits of commercial condominium ownership by an individual are discussed in further detail in this section. Such ownership is available to such individuals as doctors, dentists, lawyers, engineers, architects, businessmen, etc.

When discussing the costs of commercial space, it is important to understand that the cost figures are generally shown on a square-footage basis. If leasing space, one pays a certain dollar amount per year per square foot of usable space ($6/sq. ft./yr. to $12/sq. ft./yr.).

When purchasing commercial space, one pays a certain dollar value per square foot of space ($20/sq. ft. to $60/sq. ft.). It should be noted that the construction costs for typical office space range between $20/ to $25/sq. ft., whereas medical space ranges from $25/ to $35/sq. ft. due to the extra plumbing and partitioning requirements. But such construction cost figures are not truly representative of the purchase costs per square foot, for items such as architectural fees, engineering fees, land, construction interest, etc., must be included. Also, one must consider the efficiency of the building, Net Salable Space ÷ Gross Floor Space. If the efficiency figure of a building is 75%, and the construction cost for gross floor space including the above items is $30/sq. ft., the cost of the net salable space can be calculated as shown below.

$$\text{Cost/Sq. Ft. (Salable Space)} = \frac{\text{Cost/Sq. Ft. (Gross Floor Space)}}{\text{Efficiency}}$$

$$\text{Cost/Sq. Ft. (Salable Space)} = \frac{30/\text{Sq. Ft.}}{.75} = \$40/\text{Sq. Ft.}$$

In order to best describe the ownership responsibilities and benefits of a commercial condominium, the sample cost sheet previously referred to on page 129 will be utilized. For discussion purposes, it will be assumed that the $35,000 condominium is a 700 sq. ft. medical suite to be purchased by a physician.

The medical suite might be described as follows:

The medical condominium suite is in a new mid-rise doctors' medical office building which is located adjacent to a local hospital. The condominium unit includes a patients' waiting room, a receptionist and secretarial area, two exam treatment rooms, a small lab and storage area, a bathroom facility, and a doctor's consultation office, totaling 700 sq. ft. of net usable space. Common areas and facilities include surface parking, a modern lobby area, a pharmacy and restaurant area, and two service elevators. The building has a $30/sq. ft. construction cost for the gross floor area and a 70% space efficiency. The purchase cost per square foot of net usable space, assuming $5/sq. ft. for the added expenses previously discussed, plus the developer's profit, equals approximixately $50/sq. ft. (Purchase cost of the medical suite equals 700 sq. ft. × $50/sq. ft. = $35,000.)

The responsibilities and benefits of owning such a commercial condominium are explained under the following three headings: Initial Cash Investment, Monthly Condominium Expenses, Condominium Ownership Benefits.

Initial cash investment

The initial cash investment required when purchasing a commercial condominium generally ranges between 25% and 40% of the sales price of the condominium, which is slightly higher than the cash required for either the resort or residential condominiums. In the example shown on page 130, 30% of the $35,000 condominium is required, totaling $10,500.

Monthly condominium expenses

The monthly commercial condominium expenses include the mortgage obligation, the real estate taxes, and the maintenance fee, all of which are described below:

Mortgage obligation

The mortgage obligation available to commercial condominium owners' generally varies between 60% and 75% of the sales price of the condominium. In the example shown, a 70% mortgage commitment is assumed at an 8% rate over a 20-year period. The principal and interest payments shown have been averaged over a 10-year period and amount to a total of $2,459.16/year ($761.95+$1,697.21). Although the principal amount of the mortgage for the commercial condominium is less than that of the residential mortgage, $24,500 versus $26,250, the payments per year for the commercial condominium mortgage are greater than those of the residential mortgage ($2,459.16 versus $2,328.00) due to the higher interest rate (8% vs. 7½) and shorter term (20 years vs. 25 years) of the commercial mortgage.

Real estate taxes

The real estate tax on commercial condominiums varies according to the applicable local tax rates, and are calculated much in the same manner as those for the residential and resort condominiums. In the example shown, a yearly tax of $1,300 a year is used, which is similar to the residential condominium tax. On a per square foot basis, the yearly tax for commercial or medical space generally runs in the vicinity of $1.00 to $2.00/sq. ft./year.

Maintenance fee

The maintenance fee for a commercial condominium is somewhat higher than the fees required for residential or resort condominiums due to the daily janitorial and utility services required in the offices, as well as in the central hallways and entranceways. Such fees generally vary between $2.00/sq. ft./year to $2.50/sq. ft./year of usable space and include all janitorial services, heat and hot water, electricity, insurance, yearly audit, maintenance repairs, elevator maintenance, reserve for contingencies, and management fee. In the examples shown, a $2.15 per square foot cost is assumed for the 700-square foot office, totaling $1,510.00/year.

The total ownership costs for the example shown equals $5,269.16/year or $438.50/month, which includes the mortgage payments, the maintenance fee, and the real estate taxes.

Condominium ownership benefits

The benefits of owning a commercial condominium include tax savings, equity growth, and value appreciation, all of which are described below.

Tax benefits

The tax shelter of a commercial condominium is considerable, for not only are all expenses deductible, but depreciation may also be deducted from one's taxable income. As shown in the example, the allowable deductions include the mortgage interest, the real estate taxes, the maintenance fee, and depreciation. The depreciation has been computed on a straight line basis over 35 years. (See Appendix E for details.) The total deduction, $5,367.21, when multiplied times the physician's 40% tax bracket (slightly higher tax bracket than used in the residential example) offers a $2,146.88 tax savings per year. Such a tax savings, when subtracted from the Out-of-Pocket Costs per year equals an Effective Cost After Taxes of $3,122.28 per year or $263.00 per month.

Equity growth

The real cost of ownership takes into account the principal payments per year which should be considered an investment and not a cost. Consequently, the real cost of ownership per year equals the effective cost after tax savings less the principal payment per year which amounts to $2,360.33/year in the commercial condominium example shown.

Value appreciation

Also shown in the sample cost sheet is the potential appreciation in value of the commercial condominium over a year's period. By national standards, commercial buildings generally appreciate from 1% to 4% per year, which can amount to considerable gain during resale. As shown on the cost sheet, a 3% appreciation rate after capital gain taxes reduces the real cost of ownership by $840.00/year.

Financing a Commercial Condominium by an Organization

Commercial condominiums are not only purchased by individuals, but are also often purchased by organizations such as partnerships or corporations. The responsibilities and benefits of ownership between the different types of organizations differ slightly as briefly explained below.

Partnerships, for instance, have the same responsibilities and benefits of ownership as does the individual. Both must pay the same out-of-pocket costs before taxes and both may take the same deductions. The partners may take their share of the tax deductions against their taxable income much like that of the individual condominium owner. Both, of course, gain from equity growth and value appreciation. Commercial condominium ownership by a partnership differs from individual ownership only in that the individual partners are financially dependent upon each other.

Commercial condominium ownership by a corporation differs from ownership by an individual mainly in the area of taxation. The corporation is taxed on its profits, the individual on his personal income. Ownership deductions therefore lower taxable profit for the corporation and taxable income for the individual. The main difference between the two forms of ownership is that in order for the shareholder within the corporation to receive the net profit after taxes, the corporation must distribute the net profit after taxes as dividends. Because the shareholder must pay ordinary income taxes on the dividends, he in effect is being taxed twice.

Because there are so many types of organizations, corporations, partnerships, limited partnerships, associations, cooperatives, etc., a group of individuals should not select one type over another without consulting their tax attorney.

Analyzing the Commercial Condominium Offering

The analysis of a commercial condominium offering is no more difficult than the analysis of a residential condominium as long as the proper questions are asked. The main difference between such offerings is that the residential condominium is usually available for inspection whereas the commercial condominium is more often detailed through architectural plans. In some cases, commercial shell space may be available for inspection. It is for this reason that more descriptive questions are required when considering the purchase of commercial space. It is also important that the effective costs be recalculated for the perspective purchaser which utilizes the proper tax bracket, depreciation method, etc. Both areas are covered below.

Questioning the cost sheet data

Because most commercial condominiums are sold from shell space or architectural specifications, it is important that the purchaser be knowledgable as to exactly what he is purchasing as well as whether the cost data presented is reliable. Such information can be obtained from the following list of questions, as well as from the previous questions listed in the analysis section of the residential condominium, page 81.

1) What specific area in square feet is included in the purchase price?
2) Does such a square footage figure include a portion of the common hallway and public facilities?

3) Are there adequate specifications on the following furnishings?
   a. Heating and air conditioning—individual controls.
   b. Wall surfaces—vinyl, paint, brick, polished concrete, etc.
   c. Partitioning—type/allowance
   d. Floor covering—tile, carpet, etc.
   e. Ceiling material—suspended acoustical ceiling, plaster, etc.
   f. Bathroom facilities—both public and private areas.
4) Has the description of the landscaping work been adequately detailed?
5) Are the entranceways and hallways adequately detailed with respect to size, height, and furnishings?
6) What services are included under the maintenance fee agreement? Is the cleaning of one's office space included? Are all electrical and heating services included in the budget?
7) Is reserved parking made available with the purchase of an office suite? Are the number of spaces offered adequate to service the building?

How realistic are the effective costs?

The method in which one should view the effective costs of the commercial condominium has been previously discussed in the residential condominium section, page 82. Such considerations as interest lost on one's initial cash investment, proper application of one's tax bracket, mortgage interest deduction used, actual carrying costs and real costs of ownership, were reviewed.

A significant area that was not discussed under a residential condominium offering but should be for a commercial condominium offering is the depreciation allowance. Such a depreciation figure must be acceptable to the Internal Revenue

125

Service and should be calculated by a method which is compatible with the purchaser's reason for purchasing. For instance, one should not use a method of depreciation that depreciates the property quickly over the first few years, but much less in the later years, if he plans to own the property over the entire depreciation period. (See Appendix E for a detailed discussion of the various depreciation methods.)

The value appreciation rate/year used to determine the Effective Cost of the Resale should be related to the desirability of the offering and its location. A doctors' office building located adjacent to an expanding hospital will obviously appreciate in value faster than the same building not located near a hospital. The same holds true for the commercial retail outlet that is located in a popular shopping center rather than in a quiet suburban area.

Comparison of a Commercial Condominium Ownership Versus Rental

The advantage of purchasing commercial space rather than renting has always been questioned due to the fact that all rent payments are tax deductible. It is therefore the objective of this section to compare the purchase costs against the rental costs for comparable space so as to determine which option is most advantageous.

The $35,000 medical condominium suite previously shown on the cost sheet (page 129) is used for comparison with two rent levels shown on page 130. The higher rent level, $9.00/sq. ft./year, has been computed as the actual rent/sq. ft./year for the space being considered for purchase. The lower rent figure, $7.00/sq. ft., is only for use of comparison.

The purchase versus rental comparison shown on page 130

favors the purchase of the condominium. On a before tax basis, the Out-of-Pocket Costs/Year for the condominium are considerably lower than the Out-of-Pocket Costs for the $9.00 rental figure, even when considering the loss in interest ($525/year at 5% rate) on the initial cash payment.

The cash flow difference on an after tax basis, still favors the condominium purchase by $343/year as shown by the category Effective Cost Including Interest Lost ($3,780 less $3,437 = $343).

The main advantage to purchasing a condominiun is based on equity growth and value appreciation. As shown by the comparison, the Real Cost of Ownership which includes Equity Growth, favors condominium ownership even over the $7/sq. ft. rental figure/year. ($2,675 versus $2,940). The Actual Cost after Resale which considers potential value appreciation at a 3% rate lowers the cost/year after capital gain taxes to $1,835.

Such growth factors are more clearly shown on the following table, page 128, which is titled "Ownership Savings Over a 10 Year Period." As depicted by the table, the Ownership Savings over a $9.00/sq. ft./year rental for a 10-year period of ownership can amount to as much as $22,850 (assumes resale of the property after 10 years of ownership).

Ownership Savings Over a 10-Year Period*
($9.00/sq. ft./year Rent vs. Purchase)

Cash Outlay Saved from Purchase**	$ 3,430
Equity Buildup from Purchase***	$ 7,620
Appreciation in Value, 3%/year****	$11,800
Net Purchase Savings over Rental (10 year period)	$22,850

*   The Net Purchase Savings example assumes that all ownership operating costs and tax increases are offset by the rent increases over the 10-year period.

**   The $3,430 figure was derived from the Purchase vs. Rental Chart (page 130) previously shown. The difference in the Effective Cost including interest Lost for the $9.00/sq. ft./year rental and the Purchase Option totaled $343/year ($3,780 vs. $3,437). Over a 10-year period, the net cash savings for purchase would total $3,430.

*** The Equity Buildup figure of $7,620 was derived from the Commercial Condominium Cost Sheet, page 129, which showed an average yearly principal payment of $762 over a 10-year period. Consequently, the balance of the loan would be reduced by $762 × 10, or $7,620 over a 10-year period.

**** See Future Sales Value Chart pg. 105. Using a 3% value appreciation, the value of the medical building would be $46,800, for an appreciation in value of $11,800.

Commercial Condominium Cost Sheet
(Individual Ownership)

Sales Price	$35,000
Cash Required (30%)	$10,500
Mortgage (70%)	$24,500
Terms: 8% - 20 years	

		Yearly	Monthly
Out-of-Pocket Costs Before Taxes			
Mortgage Principal Payment		$ 761.95	$ 63.50
Mortgage Interest Payment		1,697.21	141.00
Real Estate Taxes		1,300.00	108.00
Maintenance Fee($2.25/sq. ft.)		1,510.00	126.00
Total Out-of-Pocket Costs Before Taxes		$5,269.16	$438.50
Effective Costs After Taxes			
Out-of-Pocket Costs		$5,269.16	$438.50
Less:			
Tax Savings from Deductions			
Deductions Available			
Mortgage Interest	$1,697.21		
Real Estate Taxes	1,300.00		
Maintenance Fee	1,510.00		
Depreciation	860.00		
Total Deductions	$5,367.21		
Tax Savings (40% Bracket)		2,146.88	178.50
Effective Costs After Taxes		$3,122.20	$263.00
Less: Amortization Savings		761.95	63.60
(Equity Growth)			
Real Cost of Ownership		$2,360.33	$199.40
Less: Value Appreciation (3%/year)		840.00	70.00
(After Capital Gain Taxes)			
Actual Cost after Resale		$1,520.33	$129.40
(After Taxes)			

Purchase vs. Rental
(700 sq. ft. Medical Office)

	Rental $7/sq. ft.	Actual Rental ($9/sq. ft.)	Purchase ($35,000) Mortg. $24,500 Cash Required $10,500
Out-of-Pocket Costs Before Taxes			
Rent Expense/Yr.(700 sq. ft.)	$4,900	$6,300	
Mortgage (Prin.-Int.) 8%-20 years.			$2,459
Real Estate Taxes			1,300
Maintenance Fee			1,510
Out-of-Pocket Costs/Year	$4,900	$6,300	$5,269
Out-of-Pocket Costs/Month	$ 409	$ 524	$ 438
Effective Costs After Taxes/			
Equity/Appreciation			
Out-of-Pocket Costs/Year	$4,900	$6,300	$5,269
Less: Tax Savings Deductions			

		Rental $7/sq. ft.	Actual Rental ($9/sq. ft.)	Purchase
Rental Expense	$4,900		$6,300	
Mortgage Interest				$1,697
Real Estate Taxes				1,300
Maintenance				1,510
Depreciation				860
Total Deductions	$4,900		$6,300	$5,367

	Rental $7/sq. ft.	Actual Rental ($9/sq. ft.)	Purchase
Tax Savings (40% Bracket)	1,960	2,520	2,147
Effective Cost After Taxes	2,940	3,780	$3,122
Plus: Interest Lost on Cash Pmt.	-0-	-0-	315
(After taxes)			
Effective Cost Including Int.	$2,940	$3,780	$3,437
Less: Equity Growth	-0-	-0-	762
Real Cost of Ownership	$2,940	$3,780	$2,675
Less: Value Apprec. 3%/yr.	-0-	-0-	840
(After Capital Gain Taxes)			
Actual Cost After Resale	$2,940	$3,780	$1,835
(After Taxes)			

In summary, it becomes quite obvious that the purchase of commercial space should be seriously considered. Obviously, the favorable comparison shown does not represent all commercial condominium offerings. Therefore any offering being considered must be compared with the rental option in the manner shown in the comparative example to determine whether it also favors purchase. Actual tax brackets should be used as well as local interest and appreciation rates.

This condominium buyer's guide has been written for a multitude of reasons. One was so that the public sector might gain a better understanding of the condominium way of life. Another was so that the prospective purchaser would know what questions to ask and what areas to check when analyzing an offering. Still a third was to develop a financial point of reference, so that the purchaser might compare the cost sheet of an actual offering with the samples given. But overall, the guide was written so that an interested condominium purchaser could more quickly and confidently reach a purchase decision.

Hopefully, this buyer's guide has accomplished all of the above. One may use the guide strictly as a reference tool for purchasing condominiums or as a general guide to ownership obligations and benefits. Before purchasing a condominium, the buyer should consider the steps of analysis described within the text, and might also utilize the list of questions summarized in the questionaire in Appendix A. Most important, the cost data must be thoroughly reviewed using the buyer's personal tax bracket level, mortgage requirements, and rental income objectives. Included in such analyses must be reasonable estimates of rental income, value appreciation, interest, deductions, etc.

Upon deriving one's own personal cost sheet, the monthly cost requirements before taxes must be reviewed with one's monthly budget in mind. One must not confuse such monthly cost requirements with the effective monthly costs that include yearly tax savings. Such tax savings affect the monthly costs only on a yearly basis, and then, only after monthly payments are already paid out.

Be sure to see more than one condominium offering before

making a purchase decision. Compare the advantages and disadvantages of each condominium, review their documentation, and check the reputation of both the developer and management company. If all areas for a particular offering appear favorable, the chances are good that one will enjoy the benefits of owning such a condominium.

Appendix A

Since the condominium concept of ownership was enacted on a federal level in 1961, each of the 50 states has enacted their own condominium statutes to deal most effectively with their own legislative framework. The various state statutes are basically similar as they have been based primarily on the Federal Housing Administration's Model Statute which the Federal Housing Administration regards as the best framework of condominium ownership.

Overall, the state statutes require that when a building or series of buildings is officially declared a condominium (filing of the legal documents at the Registry of Deeds), that the condominium's legal documents conform to the format stipulated in the state statutes: i.e., the declaration/master deed must include all descriptive data of the project, a schedule of each unit's proportionate interest in the common facilities, etc; the bylaws must include the establishment of the unit-owner's board of managers, the guidelines by which the unit-owner's board must rule, etc; and a list of restrictions and rules for the condominium must be attached to the master deed and bylaw documents (refer to section on legal documents—page 41).

Basically, such legal documents help protect the condominium buyer, for they require that each developer formulate a condominium offering in a workable format.

Although there are differences between the various state statutes, such differences need not be of great concern to the condominium buyer. Such differences are primarily the concern of the developer, for he must be certain that the development offering falls within the definitions and format of the specific state statute. For instance, the definition of a condominium building differs from state to state; i.e., a building containing two (2) or more units, a building containing three (3) or more units, etc. Other differences among state statutes concern the various forms of condominium ownership. For example, some states recognize commercial condominiums whereas others do not. In still other states, commercial condominiums may be recognized but must not be combined with residential ownership within the same building. Another area where state statutes differ is in the area of leasehold condominiums (retention of land ownership by the developer or by a third party). In some states, leasehold condominiums are permitted, in other states they are not. It can be concluded that the condominium buyer need only concern himself with whether the developer's offering conforms with the specific state statute. Such conformity can readily be determined by one's lawyer.

Due to the complexity and newness of the condominium ownership concept, various states have felt the need to form state regulatory agencies to oversee all condominium development so as to further protect the condominium buyer. Basically, such regulatory agencies have required that the developer report to the agency his intention to sell condominiums and to show the agency that proper steps have been taken to insure a successful development. In some states, the regulatory agency will summarize in a public report all financial and legal data pertinent to a condominium offering. Such a public report must be read by all prospective buyers before any purchase and sale agreements may be signed. It should be noted that such reports must not be construed as an approval or disapproval of the development by the regulatory agency. It is only a vehicle which the agency uses to assure that all pertinent purchase data is made available for scrutiny by the prospective buyer. In other states, condominium regulatory agencies require that the developer disclose such pertinent purchase data to all prospective buyers before any binding purchase and sale agreements are made, thereby eliminating the need for the agency to summarize such data in a public report.

Again, the basic reason for the institution of such regulatory agencies is greater buyer protection. As shown below, the states that have developed such agencies are the states where condominiums have been most popular. Effectively, the agencies force the developer to make available to the prospective buyer all development data, both legal and financial, for the buyer's inspection. Consequently, the purchase decision is based on knowledge of the facts. In those states without such condominium regulatory agencies, there is no assurance that the proper information will be made available for inspection before the purchase commitment. Although the buyer is often able to inspect the legal documentation before the signing of a purchase and sale agreement, the development's financial and cost data is most often quite limited in detail. For instance, monthly expense projections may not be backed up with detailed cost budgets, property tax estimates may not be verified by the tax assessor's office, the financial stability of the development firm may be questionable, etc. Because such data is often overlooked by condominium buyers, some buyers have found themselves as owners in developments that have ended in bankruptcy, in others that have had to raise their maintenance costs to twice what was originally projected, and still others where property taxes were not even close to original estimates.

Such disappointments have been held to a minimum by the formation of the condominium regulatory agencies which have forced developers to present all documentation, including legal, financial, and cost documents, for the prospective purchaser's inspection prior to the signing of any purchase and sale agreement.

Today, many states have already formed such regulatory agencies to protect the condominium buyer. Many other states are contemplating the formation of such agencies in the near future. Presently, some of the states utilizing such regulatory agencies or other forms of regulation include Arizona, California, Florida, Hawaii, Michigan, New York, Oregon, and Virginia.

The various forms of regulation used by the regulatory agencies of the above states vary between simple disclosure requirements of all financial and legal data to the prospective purchaser, to the strict regulation of all steps of development and marketing of a condominium offering.

A brief description of the regulatory requirements presently enacted by the above states are presented below. It should be understood that such descriptions have been written specifically for the buyer so that he may better understand how his state views condominium development. In no way should the following descriptions be used as a developer's guide to state regulations. Due to the fact that many more states are presently contemplating the formation of such regulatory agencies, prospective condominium buyers should become cognizant of such agencies when they are formed.

State Regulatory Requirements
Arizona/California/Hawaii/Oregon/Virginia

Before a condominium project may be offered for sale in the above states, a developer must notify the state condominium regulatory agency (state real estate department, real estate commission, etc.) of his intention to subdivide the land so that condominiums may be offered for sale. This notice of intention is to be accompanied by a completed questionnaire form describing the offering along with the filing fee. A simplified sample of such a questionnaire is presented later in this appendix. Upon verification of the questionnaire, an inspection of the development site may be made by the regulatory agency. If it is felt that the information submitted by the developer is sufficient for the purpose of drafting a final public report, the inspection may be waived.

The regulatory agency's final public report is to be given to all prospective purchasers for their inspection before the signing of a binding purchase and sale agreement. The report is to be presented in its complete form and cannot be changed in any manner so as to emphasize a particular area. In order to assure that each prospective purchaser has received the report, it is required that he sign a receipt for the report.

The report, as previously discussed, is not to be construed as an approval or disapproval of the development by the state regulatory agency, but is merely an informative report on the development offering to assist the prospective purchaser in reaching a more knowledgeable purchase decision. If any changes should occur after the issuance of the final report, the developer is required to request a supplementary public report to include the new information.

Michigan

The condominium regulatory process in Michigan is somewhat more rigid than the regulatory process described for the previous states. For example, along with the fact that the developer may be required to submit a detailed statement of facts about a condominium offering for the prospective buyer's inspection, the state of Michigan also requires that each step of development be approved by the regulatory agency. Such development steps are briefly described below:

1) First, if a developer wishes to test the market place for the purchase of condominiums, he must file for a permit to take reservations for purchase. Such a permit is granted by the regulatory agency upon receipt of samples of reservation documents, escrow agreements, site feasibility reports, etc.

2) Second, in order to request a permit to sell condominiums, the developer must apply for a certificate of approval of the master deed, the condominium by-laws and the subdivision plan. Upon receiving approval of such documents, the developer is required to record the master deed and bylaws with the registry of deeds, before requesting the permit to sell.

3) Lastly, in order to obtain the permit to sell condominiums, a complete set of architectural plans must be submitted to the regulatory agency for their information. If all questions as to finances, ownership, management, etc. are satisfactorily answered, the regulatory agency will approve the permit to sell condominiums which enables the developer to enter into binding purchase and sale agreements.

Basically, the above regulatory requirements make certain

that the developer has taken all necessary precautions to protect the condominium buyer. In addition, as indicated earlier, the developer might also be required to present a factual report on the development specifically for the condominium buyer's inspection. But it must be remembered that the receipt of a permit to sell condominiums does not mean that the regulatory agency approves the quality or value of the condominium offering.

New York

The State of New York requires that the condominium developer include, with all condominium sales literature, an offering plan that contains a complete summary of all development data for the prospective buyer's information. Although the offering plan is to be submitted by the developer it must conform to the guidelines specified by the regulatory agency. The information content of such an offering plan coincides closely to the information required by the sample questionnaire shown at the end of this appendix. On the front cover page of the offering plan must be a statement that indicates that the offering has neither been approved or disapproved by the Attorney General of the State of New York.

The offering plan must be filed with the Department of Law of the State of New York before the condominium development may be marketed. It should be noted that any changes in or withdrawals of the condominium offering must be recorded with the Department of Law.

Florida

As in most of the other states with regulatory agencies, Florida requires condominium developers to disclose all pertinent development data for the prospective buyer's inspection. But Florida has instituted this disclosure requirement by adding additional sections to its present condominium state statute as opposed to creating a regulatory agency.

Briefly, the statute requirement demands disclosure of the following information for the purchaser's inspection:

1) Copies of the declaration, bylaws of the condominium, and articles of incorporation of the unit-owner's organization.
2) Copy of any underlying ground leases, if any exist.
3) Copies of all budget information to include estimated monthly payments for the condominium units, estimated charges for maintenance and management of the condominium property, and monthly charges for the use of common or recreational facilities.
4) Copies of all sales literature which show the floor plans for all units being offered for purchase, as well as a description of all common facilities. An additional statement should indicate which facilities are to be owned by the unit owners and which facilities will be owned by someone other than the unit owners.

All such information is to be made available to the prospective buyer prior to the signing of a purchase and sale agreement. No changes may be made which will materially affect the rights of those buyers who have already signed binding agreements without their approval.

Sample Condominium Development Questionnaire
(Required by some state regulatory agencies)

I. Project Ownership
   a. Name and address of the developer
   b. If a partnership or corporation, give names of all members or officers and directors.

c. Names of all other individuals with a financial interest in the development
d. Names and addresses of professionals involved in the development.

Architect	. . . .
Attorney	. . . .
Contractor	. . . .
Others	. . . .

II. Project description
   a. Name of the project
   b. Location of the project
   c. Full description of the

        Land area
        Building(s)
        Units
        Common Facilities
        Recreational facilities

   d. Are all the common recreational areas and facilities to be owned by the unit-owners?

   If not, what facilities are to be retained by the developer?

   Will a fee be charged for their use? If so, how much?

   e. For what use will the property be offered?

        Single family units
        Commercial units
        Rental income
        Other

f.   What safety precautions have been included in the development?

g.   What are the scheduled completion dates for the construction of:

> Condominium housing
> Roads and sidewalks
> Recreational facilities
>> Pool
>> Tennis courts
>> Golf course
>> Community rooms
>> Other

h.   Is the development a multi-phase project?

III. Financial Information

a.   Who is financing the construction of the development?

b.   Is long term mortgage financing being made available to all prospective purchasers?

> If so, what terms are being offered and by what institution?

c.   Submit proof of financial ability to complete all improvements and facilities as indicated in the offering plan.

d.   What deposit and reservation requirements are required?

> Will all purchase reservation deposits be held in escrow?

IV. Documentation Requirements

a.   Submission of all required legal documents

> Declaration
> Bylaws and articles of organization
> Regulations and rules

b. Presentation of a schedule of all unit-owners' ownership interest in the common areas and facilities.

c. Presentation as to how the project will be taxed by the local tax assessor's office.

d. Presentation of areas and amounts of coverage by the condominium's insurance policy.

V. Agreements with all Public Agencies

    a. Water:

Is the water system completed? If not, have financial arrangements been made to ensure the system's completion?

Is the supply of water ample for adequate fire protection needs?

    b. Public Utilities:

What utilities are being made available and from what companies?

Gas ....
Electricity ....
Telephone ....

    c. Sanitation:

Is the local sewer system to be utilized? If not, show authorization from local health authorities that alternate disposal methods are acceptable.

    d. Fire Protection:

Submit letter from local fire protection agency stating that adequate fire protection will be provided.

e. Streets and Roads:

Are the streets public streets? If not, what provisions have been made for the repair and maintenance of the private roads?

VI. Management and Operation Services
   a. Who will initially manage and maintain the common facilities of the condominium development?
   b. At what point of time will the management duties be transferred to the organization of unit-owners?
   c. What is the yearly budget protection for the maintenance and operation of the condominium development, including, but not limited to, the following:

Operational Costs

Utilities (Elec., water, telephone, etc.)
Heating fuels (Gas, oil, elec.)
Janitorial and cleaning services
Trash and garbage disposal services
Ground and building maintenance services
Other operating services

Management Costs

Legal and accounting services
Management fee
Other management costs

Fixed Costs

Building Insurance
Elevator maintenance
Other fixed costs

Reserve Costs

> Reserve for unexpected repair work
> Reserve for replacement of common area
>   carpets, furniture, etc.
> Reserve for improvements and alterations
>   to common facilities
> Other reserve funds

   d. If an insufficient number of units are sold to cover the proposed operations budget at the stated unit monthly fee projections, what provisions have been made to provide for the deficit?

VII. Sales Plan

   a. Name of sales agency(s) or broker(s) handling sales.

   b. Submit all brochures, proposed advertisements, and sales material.

   c. Submit all documents describing the terms and conditions of sale, and all escrow agreements.

   d. Will any special sales inducements be used in the sales program?

> Club memberships
> Free inspection trips
> Money back guarantees
> Reductions in price under special conditions
> Other inducements

VIII. General Area Information

   a. Transportation:

> What public transportation is available to the proposed condominium development?

b. Schools:

What public and private schools are in the vicinity of the development? Will school bus service be made available?

c. Shopping Areas:

How close are the nearest shopping facilities to the development?

Appendix B

MODEL FEDERAL HOUSING AUTHORITY
CONDOMINIUM STATUTE

Section 1: Apartment Ownership Act. This Act shall be known as the "Apartment Ownership Act."

Section 2: Definitions. As used in this Act, unless the context otherwise requires:

(a) "Apartment" means a part of the property intended for any type of independent use, including one or more rooms or enclosed spaces located on one or more floors (or part or parts thereof) in a building, and with a direct exit to a public street or highway or to a common area leading to such street or highway.

(b) "Apartment owner" means the person or persons owning an apartment in fee simple absolute and an undivided interest in the fee simple estate of the common areas and facilities in the percentage specified and established in the Declaration.

(c) "Apartment number" means the number, letter, or combination thereof, designating the apartment in the Declaration.

(d) "Association of apartment owners" means all of the apartment owners acting as a group in accordance with the By-laws and Declaration.

(e) "Building" means a building, containing five or more apartments, or two or more buildings, each containing two or more apartments, with a total of five or more apartments for all such buildings, and comprising a part of the property.

(f) "Common areas and facilities," unless otherwise provided in the Declaration or lawful amendments thereto, means and includes:

(1) The land on which the building is located;

(2) The foundations, columns, girders, beams, supports, main walls, roofs, halls, corridors, lobbies, stairs, stairways, fire escapes, and entrances and exits of the building;

(3) The basements, yards, gardens, parking areas and storage spaces;

(4) The premises for the lodging of janitors or persons in charge of the property;

(5) Installations of central services such as power, light, gas, hot and cold water, heating, refrigeration, air conditioning and incinerating;

(6) The elevators, tanks, pumps, motors, fans, compressors, ducts and in general all apparatus and installations existing for common use;

(7) Such community and commercial facilities as may be provided for in the Declaration; and

(8) All other parts of the property necessary or convenient to its existence, maintenance and safety, or normally in common use.

(g) "Common expenses" means and include:

(1) All sums lawfully assessed against the apartment owners by the Association of Apartment Owners;

(2) Expenses of administration, maintenance, repair or replacement of the common areas and facilities;

(3) Expenses agreed upon as common expenses by the Association of Apartment Owners;

(4) Expenses declared common expenses by provisions of this Act, or by the Declaration or the By-laws.

(h) "Common profits" means the balance of all income, rents, profits and revenues from the common areas and facilities remaining after the deduction of the common expenses.

(i) "Declaration" means the instrument by which the property is submitted to the provisions of this Act, as hereinafter provided, and such Declaration as from time to time may be lawfully amended.

(j) "Limited common areas and facilities" means and include those common areas and facilities designated in the Declaration as reserved for use of certain apartment or apartments to the exclusion of the other apartments.

(k) "Majority" or "Majority of apartment owners" means the apartment owners with 51% or more of the votes in accordance with the percentages assigned in the Declaration to the apartments for voting purposes.

149

(l)   "Person" means individual, corporation, partnership, association, trustee or other legal entity.

(m)   "Property" means and includes the land, the building, all improvements and structures thereon, all owned in fee simple absolute and all easements, rights and appurtenances belonging thereto, and all articles of personal property intended for use in connection therewith, which have been or are intended to be submitted to the provisions of the Act.

Section 3: Application of Act. This Act shall be applicable only to property, the sole owner or all of the owners of which submit the same to the provisions hereof by duly executing and recording a Declaration as hereinafter provided.

Section 4: Status of the Apartments. Each apartment, together with its undivided interest in the common areas and facilities, shall for all purposes constitute real property.

Section 5: Ownership of Apartments. Each apartment owner shall be entitled to the exclusive ownership and possession of his apartment.

Section 6: Common Areas and Facilities.

(a)   Each apartment owner shall be entitled to an undivided interest in the common areas and facilities in the percentage expressed in the Declaration. Such percentage shall be computed by taking as a basis the value of the apartment in relation to the value of the property.

(b)   The percentage of the undivided interest of each apartment owner in the common areas and facilities as expressed in the Declaration shall have a permanent character and shall not be altered without the consent of all of the apartment owners expressed in an amended Declaration duly recorded. The percentage of the undivided interest in the common areas and facilities shall not be separated from the apartment to which it appertains and shall be deemed to be conveyed or encumbered with the apartment even though such interest is not expressly mentioned or described in the conveyance or other instrument.

(c)   The common areas and facilities shall remain undivided and no apartment owner or any other person shall bring any action for partition or division of any part thereof, unless the property has been removed from the provisions of this Act as provided in Sections 16 and 26. Any covenant to the contrary shall be null and void.

(d)   Each apartment owner may use the common areas and facilities in accordance with the purpose for which they were intended without hindering or encroaching upon the lawful rights of the other apartment owners.

(e)   The necessary work of maintenance, repair and replacement of the common areas and facilities and the making of any additions or improvements thereto shall be carried out only as provided herein and in the By-laws.

(f) The Association of Apartment Owners shall have the irrevocable right, to be exercised by the Manager or Board of Directors, to have access to each apartment from time to time during reasonable hours as may be necessary for the maintenance, repair or replacement of any of the common areas and facilities therein or accessible therefrom, or for making emergency repairs therein necessary to prevent damage to the common areas and facilities or to another apartment or apartments.

Section 7: Compliance with Covenants, By-laws and Administrative Provisions. Each apartment owner shall comply strictly with the by-laws and with the administrative rules and regulations adopted pursuant thereto, as either of the same may be lawfully amended from time to time, and with the covenants, conditions and restrictions set forth in the declaration or in the deed to his apartment. Failure to comply with any of the same shall be ground for an action to recover sums due, for damages or injunctive relief or both maintainable by the manager or Board of Directors on behalf of the Association of Apartment Owners or, in a proper case, by an aggrieved apartment owner.

Section 8: Certain Work Prohibited. No apartment owner shall do any work which would jeopardize the soundness or safety of the property, reduce the value thereof or impair any easement or hereditament without in every such case the unanimous consent of all the other apartment owners being first obtained.

Section 9: Liens Against Apartments; Removal from Lien; Effect of Part Payment.

(a) Subsequent to recording the Declaration as provided in this Act, and while the property remains subject to this Act, no lien shall thereafter arise or be effective against the property. During such period liens or encumbrances shall arise or be created only against each apartment and the percentage of undivided interest in the common areas and facilities, appurtenant to such apartment, in the same manner and under the same conditions in every respect as liens or encumbrances may arise or be created upon or against any other separate parcel of real property subject to individual ownership; Provided that no labor performed or materials furnished with the consent or at the request of an apartment owner or his agent or his contractor or subcontractor, shall be the basis for the filing of a lien pursuant to the Lien Law against the apartment or any other property of any other apartment owner not expressly consenting to or requesting the same, except that such express consent shall be deemed

151

to be given by the owner of any apartment in the case of emergency repairs thereto. Labor performed or material furnished for the common areas and facilities, if duly authorized by the Association of Apartment Owners, the Manager or Board of Directors in accordance with this Act, the Declaration or By-laws, shall be deemed to be performed or furnished with the express consent of each apartment owner and shall be the basis for the filing of a lien pursuant to the Lien Law against each of the apartments and shall be subject to the provisions of subparagraph (b) hereunder.

(b)   In the event a lien against two or more apartments becomes effective, the apartment owners of the separate apartments may remove their apartment and the percentage of undivided interest in the common areas and facilities appurtenant to such apartment from the lien by payment of the fractional or proportional amounts attributable to each of the apartments affected. Such individual payment shall be computed by reference to the percentages appearing on the Declaration. Subsequent to any such payment, discharge or other satisfaction the apartment and the percentage of undivided interest in the common areas and facilities appurtenant thereto shall thereafter be free and clear of the lien so paid, satisfied or discharged. Such partial payment, satisfaction or discharge shall not prevent the lienor from proceeding to enforce his rights against any apartment and the percentage of undivided interest in the common areas and facilities appurtenant thereto not so paid, satisfied or discharged.

Section 10: Common Profits and Expenses. The common profits of the property shall be distributed among, and the common expenses shall be charged to, the apartment owners according to the percentage of the undivided interest in the common areas and facilities.

Section 11: Contents of Declaration. The declaration shall contain the following particulars:

1.   Description of the land on which the building and improvements are or are to be located.

2.   Description of the building, stating the number of stories and basements, the number of apartments and the principal materials of which it is or is to be constructed.

3.   The apartment number of each apartment, and a statement of its location, approximate area, number of rooms, and immediate common area to which it has access, and any other data necessary for its proper identification.

4. Description of the common areas and facilities.

5. Description of the limited common areas and facilities, if any, stating to which apartments their use is reserved.

6. Value of the property and of each apartment, and the percentage of undivided interest in the common areas and facilities appertaining to each apartment and its owner for all purposes, including voting.

7. Statement of the purposes for which the building and each of the apartments are intended and restricted as to use.

8. The name of a person to receive service of process in the cases hereinafter provided, together with the residence or place of business of such person which shall be within the city or county in which the building is located.

9. Provision as to the percentage of votes by the apartment owners which shall be determinative of whether to rebuild, repair, restore, or sell the property in the event of damage or destruction of all or part of the property.

10. Any further details in connection with the property which the person executing the Declaration may deem desirable to set forth consistent with this Act.

11. The method by which the Declaration may be amended, consistent with the provisions of this Act.

Section 12: Contents of Deeds of Apartments. Deeds of apartments shall include the following particulars:

1. Description of the land as provided in Section 11 of this Act, or the post office address of the property, including in either case the liber, page and date of recording of the Declaration.

2. The apartment number of the apartment in the Declaration and any other data necessary for its proper identification.

3. Statement of the use for which the apartment is intended and restrictions on its use.

4. The percentage of undivided interest appertaining to the apartment in the common areas and facilities.

5. Any further details which the grantor and grantee may deem desirable to set forth consistent with the Declaration and this Act.

Section 13: Copy of the Floor Plans to Be Filed. Simultaneously with the recording of the Declaration there shall be filed in the office of the recording officer a set of the floor plans of the building showing the layout, location, apartment numbers and dimensions of the apartments, stating the name of the building or that it has no name, and bearing the verified statement of a registered architect or licensed professional engineer certifying that it is an

153

accurate copy of portions of the plans of the building as filed with and approved by the municipal or other governmental subdivision having jurisdiction over the issuance of permits for the construction of buildings. If such plans do not include a verified statement by such architect or engineer that such plans fully and accurately depict the layout, location, apartment numbers and dimensions of the apartments as built, there shall be recorded prior to the first conveyance of any apartment an amendment to the Declaration to which shall be attached a verified statement of a registered architect or licensed professional engineer certifying that the plans theretofore filed, or being filed simultaneously with such amendment, fully and accurately depict the layout, location, apartment numbers and dimensions of the apartments as built. Such plans shall be kept by the recording officer in a separate file for each building, indexed in the same manner as a conveyance entitled to record, numbered serially in the order of receipt, each designated "apartment ownership," with the name of the building, if any, and each containing a reference to the liber, page and date of recording of the Declaration. Correspondingly, the record of the Declaration shall contain a reference to the file number of the floor plans of the building affected thereby.

Section 14: Blanket Mortgages and Other Blanket Liens Affecting an Apartment at Time of First Conveyance. At the time of the first conveyance of each apartment, every mortgage and other lien affecting such apartment, including the percentage of undivided interest of the apartment in the common areas and facilities, shall be paid and satisfied of record, or the apartment being conveyed and its percentage of undivided interest in the common areas and facilities shall be released therefrom by partial release duly recorded.

Section 15: Recording.

(a) The Declaration, any amendment or amendments thereof, any instrument by which the provisions of this Act may be waived, and every instrument affecting the property or any apartment shall be entitled to be recorded. Neither the Declaration nor any amendment thereof shall be valid unless duly recorded.

(b) In addition to the records and indexes required to be maintained by the recording officer, the recording officer shall maintain an index or indexes whereby the record of each Declaration contains a reference to the record of each conveyance of an apartment affected by such Declaration, and the record of each conveyance of an apartment contains a reference to the Declaration of the building of which such apartment is a part.

Section 16: Removal From Provisions of This Act.

(a) All of the apartment owners may remove a property from the provisions of this Act by an instrument to that effect, duly recorded, provided that the holders of all liens affecting any of the apartments consent thereto or agree, in either case by instruments duly recorded, that their liens be transferred to the percentage of the undivided interest of the apartment owner in the property as hereinafter provided.

(b) Upon removal of the property from the provisions of this Act, the property shall be deemed to be owned in common by the apartment owners. The undivided interest in the property owned in common which shall appertain to each apartment owner shall be the percentage of undivided interest previously owned by such owner in the common areas and facilities.

Section 17: Removal No Bar to Subsequent Resubmission. The removal provided for in the preceding section shall in no way bar the subsequent resubmission of the property to the provisions of this Act.

Section 18: By-laws. The administration of every property shall be governed by by-laws, a true copy of which shall be annexed to the Declaration and made a part thereof. No modification of or amendment to the by-laws shall be valid unless set forth in an amendment to the Declaration and such amendment is duly recorded.

Section 19: Contents of By-laws. The by-laws may provide for the following:

(a) The election from among the apartment owners of a Board of Directors, the number of persons constituting the same, and that the terms of at least one-third of the Directors shall expire annually; the powers and duties of the Board; the compensation, if any, of the Directors; the method of removal from office of Directors; and whether or not the Board may engage the services of a manager or managing agent.

(b) Method of calling meetings of the apartment owners; what percentage, if other than a majority of apartment owners shall constitute a quorum.

(c) Election of a President from among the Board of Directors who shall preside over the meetings of the Board of Directors and of the Association of Apartment Owners.

(d) Election of a Secretary who shall keep the minute book wherein resolutions shall be recorded.

(e) Election of a Treasurer who shall keep the financial records and books of account.

(f) Maintenance, repair and replacement of the common areas and facilities and payments therefor, including the method of approving payment vouchers.

(g)   Manner of collecting from the apartment owners their share of the common expenses.

(h)   Designation and removal of personnel necessary for the maintenance, repair and replacement of the common areas and facilities.

(i)   Method of adopting and of amending administrative rules and regulations governing the details of the operation and use of the common areas and facilities.

(j)   Such restrictions on the requirements respecting the use and maintenance of the apartments and the use of the common areas and facilities, not set forth in the Declaration, as are designed to prevent unreasonable interference with the use of their respective apartments and of the common areas and facilities by the several apartment owners.

(k)   The percentage of votes required to amend the By-laws.

(l)   Other provisions as may be deemed necessary for the administration of the property consistent with this Act.

Section 20: Books of Receipts and Expenditures; Availability for Examination. The manager or Board of Directors, as the case may be, shall keep detailed, accurate records in chronological order, of the receipts and expenditures affecting the common areas and facilities, specifying and itemizing the maintenance and repair expenses of the common areas and facilities and any other expenses incurred. Such records and the vouchers authorizing the payments shall be available for examination by the apartment owners at convenient hours of week days.

Section 21: Waiver of Use of Common Areas and Facilities; Abandonment of Apartment. No apartment owner may exempt himself from liability for his contribution towards the common expenses by waiver of the use or enjoyment of any of the common areas and facilities or by abandonment of his apartment.

Section 22: Separate Taxation. Each apartment and its percentage of undivided interest in the common areas and facilities shall be deemed to be a parcel and shall be subject to separate assessment and taxation by each assessing unit and special district for all types of taxes authorized by law including but not limited to special ad valorem levies and special assessments. Neither the building, the property nor any of the common areas and facilities shall be deemed to be a parcel.

Section 23: Priority of Lien.

(a)   All sums assessed by the Association of Apartment Owners but unpaid for the share of the common expenses chargeable to any apartment shall constitute a lien on such apartment prior to all other liens except only (i) tax liens on the apartment in favor of any assessing unit and special district, and (ii) all sums unpaid on a first mortgage of record. Such lien may be foreclosed by suit by the manager or Board of Directors, acting on behalf of the apartment owners, in like manner as a mortgage of real property. In any such foreclosure the apartment owner shall be required to pay a reasonable rental for the apartment, if so provided in the by-laws, and the plaintiff in such foreclosure shall be entitled to the appointment of a receiver to collect the same. The manager or Board of Directors, acting on behalf of the apartment owners, shall have power, unless prohibited by the declaration, to bid in the apartment at foreclosure sale, and to acquire and hold, lease, mortgage and convey the same. Suit to recover a money judgment for unpaid common expenses shall be maintainable without foreclosing or waiving the lien securing the same.

(b) Where the mortgagee of a first mortgage of record or other purchaser of an apartment obtains title to the apartment as a result of foreclosure of the first mortgage, such acquirer of title, his successors and assigns, shall not be liable for the share of the common expenses or assessments by the Association of Apartment Owners chargeable to such apartment which became due prior to the acquisition of title to such apartment by such acquirer. Such unpaid share of common expenses or assessments shall be deemed to be common expenses collectible from all of the apartment owners including such acquirer, his successors and assigns.

Section 24: Joint and Several Liability of Grantor and Grantee for Unpaid Common Expenses. In a voluntary conveyance the grantee of an apartment shall be jointly and severally liable with the grantor for all unpaid assessments against the latter for his share of the common expenses up to the time of the grant or conveyance, without prejudice to the grantee's right to recover from the grantor the amounts paid by the grantee therefor. However, any such grantee shall be entitled to a statement from the manager or Board of Directors, as the case may be, setting forth the amount of the unpaid assessments against the grantor and such grantee shall not be liable for, nor shall the apartment conveyed be subject to a lien for, any unpaid assessments against the grantor in excess of the amount therein set forth.

Section 25: Insurance. The manager or the Board of Directors, if required by the declaration, by-laws or by a majority of the apartment owners, or at the request of a mortgagee having a first mortgage of record covering an apartment, shall have the authority to, and shall, obtain insurance for the property against loss or damage by fire and such other hazards under such terms and

157

for such amounts as shall be required or requested. Such insurance coverage shall be written on the property in the name of such manager or of the Board of Directors of the Association of Apartment Owners, as trustee for each of the apartment owners in the percentages established in the declaration. Premiums shall be common expenses. Provision for such insurance shall be without prejudice to the right of each apartment owner to insure his own apartment for his benefit.

Section 26: Disposition of Property; Destruction or Damage. If, within . . . . days of the date of the damage or destruction to all or part of the property, it is not determined by the Association of Apartment Owners to repair, reconstruct or rebuild, then and in that event:

(a)   The property shall be deemed to be owned in common by the apartment owners;

(b)   The undivided interest in the property owned in common which shall appertain to each apartment owner shall be the percentage of undivided interest previously owned by such owner in the common areas and facilities;

(c)   Any liens affecting any of the apartments shall be deemed to be transferred in accordance with the existing priorities to the percentage of the undivided interest of the apartment owner in the property as provided herein; and

(d)   The property shall be subject to an action for partition at the suit of any apartment owner, in which event the net proceeds of sale, together with the net proceeds of the insurance on the property, if any, shall be considered as one fund and shall be divided among all the apartment owners in a percentage equal to the percentage of undivided interest owned by each owner in the property, after first paying out of the respective shares of the apartment owners, to the extent sufficient for the purpose, all liens on the undivided interest in the property owned by each apartment owner.

Section 27: Actions. Without limiting the rights of any apartment owner, actions may be brought by the manager or Board of Directors, in either case in the discretion of the Board of Directors, on behalf of two or more of the apartment owners, as their respective interests may appear, with respect to any cause of action relating to the common areas and facilities or more than one apartment. Service of process on two or more apartment owners in any action relating to the common areas and facilities or more than one apartment may be made on the person designated in the Declaration to receive service of process.

158

Section 28: Personal Application.

(a)   All apartment owners, tenants of such owners, employees of owners and tenants, or any other persons that may in any manner use property or any part thereof submitted to the provisions of this Act shall be subject to this Act and to the Declaration and By-laws of the Association of Apartment Owners adopted pursuant to the provisions of this Act.

(b)   All agreements, decisions and determinations lawfully made by the Association of Apartment Owners in accordance with the voting percentages established in the Act, Declaration or By-laws, shall be deemed to be binding on all apartment owners.

Section 29: Severability. If any provision of this Act or any section, sentence, clause, phrase or word, or the application thereof in any circumstance is held invalid, the validity of the remainder of the Act and of the application of any such provision, section, sentence, clause, phrase or word in any other circumstances shall not be affected thereby.

Appendix C

SAMPLE LEGAL DOCUMENTATION

There is attached to this covering memorandum the following documents concerning the condominium apartment unit in the state of Massachusetts in which you have expressed an interest:

1.   Purchase and Sale Agreement covering the unit.
2.   Master Deed of the *(project name)* Condominium.
3.   Form of Unit Deed.
4.   *(Project name)* Condominium Trust.

Condominium ownership carries with it the tax advantages of home ownership without the disadvantages of maintenance concerns. A condominium owner owns his apartment plus a percentage interest in the common areas and facilities of the condominium, such as the condominium land, the common recreational facilities and the common areas of the condominium building or buildings. The Master Deed is the document which establishes the condominium. Condominium ownership is acquired by means of the Unit Deed. Each unit owner can re-sell his unit, subject to the right of first refusal in the Board of Trustees of the Condominium Trust. The unit owner can mortgage his unit irrespective of whether other unit owners do. He can decorate the

159

interior of the unit as he sees fit. The Condominium Trust is the vehicle through which the Board of Trustees chosen by the unit owners operates and manages the condominium. The cost of that operation and maintenance is shared by the individual unit owners in proportion to their respective interests in the common facilities, which proportion is set forth in such owner's Unit Deed.

EDITORS NOTE: The following documents are prepared for the State of Massachusetts; however, they are essentially the same as those used throughout the United States.

PURCHASE AND SALE AGREEMENT

This agreement is made this __ day of _____, 197 , between *(sellers)*, *(hereinafter called "Seller")* and . . . .

of

(hereinafter called "Buyer"),

WITNESSETH:

WHEREAS, Seller is the owner of premises at *(location)*, and Seller intends to build thereon *(amount)* apartment buildings, and intends to record a master condominium deed in accordance with Chapter 183A of the Massachusetts General Laws and to establish an organization of unit owners in accordance with Section 10 of Chapter 183A;

WHEREAS, Buyer desires to purchase a condominium unit in said premises to be known as *(project name)* Condominium for use as a residence, together with an undivided interest in the common areas and facilities of said premises;

NOW, THEREFORE, in consideration of the mutual promises herein contained, Seller and Buyer agree as follows:

1. *Purchase Price and Deposit.* The Buyer agrees to purchase Unit in *(project name)* Condominium as shown substantially on a plan dated _____, for the price of _____ DOLLARS, of which _____ DOLLARS have been paid as a deposit this day, and the balance is to be paid upon delivery of the deed of said Unit, such balance to be paid in cash or by certified or bank cashier's or treasurer's check payable to the Seller. The deposit paid under this Section 1 shall be held by the Seller in a segregated trust account in *(name)* Bank, for the benefit of condominium buyers until the condition on Seller's obligations set forth in Section 19 is satisfied. When such condition is satisfied, the Seller may use the deposit in connection with the construction of said buildings. In the event that the Seller cancels its obligations hereunder pursuant to the provisions of Section 19, the Seller shall return the Buyer's deposit. If the Buyer shall fail to fulfill the Buyer's agreements herein, the Buyer's deposit shall be retained by the Seller as liquidated damages, unless within thirty (30) days after the time for performance of this agreement or any extension hereof, the Seller otherwise notifies the Buyer in writing.

The share of the Buyer's Unit in the common areas and facilities of the condominium is   percent.

2. *Action on Buyer's Offer.* Upon execution of this instrument by the Seller and the delivery of a fully-executed copy thereof to the Buyer, this agreement shall become and constitute a mutually binding purchase and sale agreement between the Seller and Buyer, subject only to the condition on Seller's obligation set forth in Section 19 hereof.

3. *Delivery of Unit Deed.* Seller shall on or before   convey to the Buyer, or a nominee designated by the Buyer, and approved by the Seller at

least seven (7) days prior to the closing date, said Unit together with the undivided interest appertaining to the Unit in the common areas and facilities in *(project name)* Condominium by a good and sufficient quitclaim deed complying with the provisions of Massachusetts General Laws, Chapter 183A, Section 9, conveying a good and clear record and marketable title thereto, free of encumbrances except:

(a) (i) Provisions of said Chapter 183A; (ii) the Master Deed establishing said condominium, a copy of which the Buyer acknowledges has been furnished to the Buyer; (iii) the Declaration of Trust establishing the condominium trust which will own and manage the common areas and facilities, the By-Laws set forth therein and any rules and regulations promulgated thereunder, a copy of which the Buyer acknowledges has been furnished to the Buyer; and (iv) any contracts for building maintenance services entered into by the Seller or the condominium trust with third persons and the obligations thereunder to pay the proportionate share of such expenses attributable to said Unit after the delivery of the deed, which the Buyer shall agree to perform and assume. The Master Deed and Declaration of Trust shall be recorded substantially in the same form and content as the documents furnished to the Buyer, but may be altered in small degree upon request of counsel for an institutional mortgage lender but in no way as will materially prejudice a Unit owner;

(b) Rights, easements and restrictions of record, none of which prevent or interfere with the use and enjoyment of the Unit and the building in which the Unit is situated for residential purposes;

(c) Provisions of existing building and zoning laws;

(d) Such taxes attributable to said Unit for the then current year as are not due and payable on the date of delivery of such deed.

4. *Closing Date.* The Seller shall deliver the Unit deed to the Buyer at the *(place)* Registry of Deeds at *(time)* on the Closing Date designated by the seller by notice to the Buyer. The Closing Date shall be (a) not sooner than thirty (30) days after the recording of said Master Deed; and (b) not sooner than thirty (30) days nor more than sixty (60) days after the date on which said notice is given, unless otherwise agreed upon in writing. The Closing Date shall in all events, but subject to the provisions of Section 8 hereof, be not later than the date set forth in Section 3 hereof. It is agreed that time is of the essence hereof.

5. *Available Mortgage Financing. (name)* Bank has indicated its willingness to provide first mortgage financing for the purchase of condominium units in *(name)* Condominium. Loans will be written up to   percent of the Unit sales price stipulated in Section 1, but not to exceed   , at said bank's prevailing interest rates for condominium loans at the time of loan application. Each Unit loan shall be subject to financing charges and credit

approvals. The preceding two sentences are purely informational and are not an offer by the Seller to arrange for the extension of credit. The Buyer shall have the right to arrange for a mortgage loan with any other banking source or to use the Buyer's own resources, provided, however, that the Buyer agrees that if Buyer seeks mortgage financing, Buyer will apply for a mortgage loan at *(name)* Bank and to accept the same unless Buyer obtains a loan committment from another lending institution on more favorable terms.

6. *Possession.* The Seller shall deliver full possession of the Unit free of all tenants and occupants on the Closing Date, said Unit to be then (a) substantially completed, (b) not in violation of building and zoning laws of the City of _____; and (c) in compliance with the provisions of any instrument referred to in Section 3 hereof. The common areas and facilities shall be sufficiently completed on the Closing Date as to make occupancy of the Unit practicable.

7. *Extension to Perfect Title or Make Premises Conform.* If the Seller shall be unable to give title or to make conveyence, or to deliver possession of the Unit as herein provided on or before the date set forth in Section 3, or at the Closing Date specified by the Seller's notice under Section 4, or if at the time of the delivery of the deed the Unit does not conform with the provisions hereof, then any deposits made under this agreement shall be refunded, and all other obligations of the parties hereto shall cease, and this agreement shall be void and without recourse to the parties hereto. Seller shall, at the Buyer's written request, use reasonable efforts to remove any defects in title, or to deliver possession as provided herein, or to make the said Unit conform to the provisions hereof, as the case may be. To enable the Seller so to do, the time for performance hereunder shall be extended for a period designated by the Seller, not in excess of sixty (60) days. At the expiration of the extended time, if the Seller shall have failed so to remove any defects in title, deliver possession, or make the Unit conform, as the case may be, all as herein agreed, then at the Buyer's option, any payments made under this agreement shall be forthwith refunded and all other obligations of all parties hereto shall cease and this agreement shall be void without recourse to the parties hereto. The Buyer shall have the election, at either the original or any extended time for performance, to accept such title as the Seller can deliver to the Unit in its then condition and to pay therefor the purchase price without deduction, in which case the Seller shall convey such title.

8. *Force Majeure.* If the Seller shall be delayed, hindered in, or prevented from the performance of any act required hereunder by reason of strikes, inability to procure materials, restrictive governmental regulations, riots, war, flood or other reason beyond the Seller's control, then the time for the Seller's performance hereunder shall be extended for a period equivalent to the period of such delay; provided, however, if such delays prevent the Seller from

163

performing its obligations hereunder by *(date)*, the Buyer may cancel Buyer's obligations hereunder and shall in that event be entitled to a return of the Buyer's deposit.

9. *Agreement Merged in Deed.* The acceptance of a deed by the Buyer shall be deemed to be a full performance and discharge of every agreement and obligation herein contained or expressed, except such as are, by the term hereof, to be performed after the delivery of said deed.

10. *Use of Purchase Money to Clear Title.* To enable the Seller to make conveyance as herein provided, the Seller may, at the time of delivery of the deed, use the purchase money or any portion thereof to clear the title of any or all encumbrances or interests, provided that all instruments so procured are recorded simultaneously with the delivery of said deed or satisfactory arrangements are made for subsequent recording.

11. *Insurance.* Until the delivery of the deed, the Seller (or the condominium trust) shall maintain fire and extended coverage insurance on the building in which said Unit is located as now in force. It is the intention of the Seller that the condominium trust will maintain insurance policies covering the buildings against loss by fire and other hazards included in extended coverage and to insure the trust and Unit owners against public liability, and that the cost of maintaining this insurance will be charged to the Unit owners in accordance with their respective percentage interests from the time they respectively acquire title. Such insurance coverage will be without prejudice to the right of any Unit owner to purchase supplemental insurance.

12. *Adjustments.* Taxes for the then current year, service contract payments, and pre-paid insurance premiums allocable to the Buyer's unit and the Buyer's proportionate share of common areas and facilities, and other common charges such as management charges, whether pre-paid by the Seller or the condominium trust, shall be apportioned as of the day of performance of this agreement, and the net amount thereof shall be added to or deducted from, as the case may be, the purchase price payable by the Buyer at the time of delivery of the deed. If, during the year the closing takes place, *(name)* Condominium is not assessed as a condominium, the Buyer will pay to the Seller a pro rata portion of the taxes for such year so that the Seller may pay the entire tax bill for that year. If the amount of said taxes is not known at the time of the delivery of the deed, they shall be apportioned in accordance with the share of said Unit in the common areas and facilities, and on the basis of the taxes assessed for the preceding year, with a reapportionment as soon as the new tax rate and valuation can be ascertained; and, if the taxes which are to be apportioned shall thereafter be reduced by abatement, the amount of such abatement, less the reasonable cost of obtaining the same, shall be apportioned between the parties, provided that neither party shall be obli-

gated to institute or prosecute proceedings for an abatement unless herein otherwise agreed.

13. *Broker's Commission.* Except as hereinafter provided, no commission with respect to the transactions hereunder shall be paid by the Seller, and the Buyer represents that he was not introduced to the Seller or the premises, or induced to enter into this agreement, by any broker; provided, however, that a commission as agreed shall be paid, if and when the deed is delivered and the purchase price is paid, by the Seller/Buyer to the following broker:

14. *First Deposit to Condominium Trust Fund.* At the time of delivery of the Unit deed, the Buyer will deposit with the (*name*) Condominium Trust one-quarter (1/4) of the estimated annual common facilities charges allocable to the Buyer's Unit to provide the Condominium with working capital and a contingency reserve. The common facilities charges include, without implied limitation, general repairs and maintenance, electricity, water, insurance, sewer, legal and accounting fees, and management charges.

15. *Assignment to Condominium Trust.* The Seller may assign its rights and obligations hereunder to the (*name*) Condominium Trust.

16. *Title Reference.* For the Seller's title, see the following deeds:

17. *Unsold Units.* The Seller reserves the right in order to facilitate the marketing of units and to accommodate the actual cost of improvements to raise or lower the prices of unsold units, or to make such modifications, additions or deletions in or to, the Master Deed or the Declaration of Trust establishing the condominium trust as may be approved or required by any lending institution designated by the Seller to make mortgage loans on units, or by public authorities provided that none of the foregoing shall:

(a) Increase the price of the unit being sold hereunder;

(b) Diminish or increase the percentage of undivided interest and the voting rights of the unit being sold hereunder; and

(c) Diminish or increase the percentage of undivided interest and the voting rights of units already sold.

18. *Management.* The Seller may cause to be provided supervisory management by a real estate management company at market rates for one year after the Master Deed is recorded.

19. *Number of Units Sold.* If by _____, the aggregate dollar value of the purchase prices of Units which the Seller has under signed purchase and sale agreements is not at least fifty (50) percent of the aggregate dollar value of the purchase prices submitted to Buyer of all the units in the condominium, the Seller may cancel its obligations hereunder and shall in that event refund the Buyer's deposit without interest.

20. *Notice.* Any notice hereunder shall be deemed to have been duly given if in writing and mailed by registered or certified mail, return receipt requested, all charges prepaid, addressed, in the case of the Buyer, to the Buyer

named at the address designated above, and in the case of the Seller to: *(address)*. Either party may notify the other by such notice of a new address, in which case such new address shall be employed for all subsequent mailings to make conveyance as herein provided.

21.   *Projections.* Information furnished to the Buyer concerning taxes and operating expenses of the condominium is estimated by Seller in good faith on the best information available to Seller, but the Seller does not warrant the accuracy of projections or expectations. The Seller also expressly disclaims any representations or warranties not expressly made in this agreement in writing.

22.   *Construction of Agreement.* This instrument, executed in triplicate, is to be construed as a Massachusetts contract, is to take effect as a sealed instrument and sets forth the entire contract between the parties. It shall be binding upon the respective heirs, devisees, executors, administrators, successors and assigns of the parties, and may be cancelled, modified or amended only by a written instrument executed by both the Seller and the Buyer. Captions before each section are for convenience of reference only and shall be of no effect in the construction of this instrument.

WITNESS the execution hereof under seal the day and year first above written.

SELLER:

_____

BUYER:

_____

MASTER DEED
OF THE
(name) CONDOMINIUM

We, *(name)*, (hereinafter called "the Grantors"), the sole owners of the premises in Massachusetts, hereinafter described, by duly executing and recording this Master Deed, do hereby submit said premises to the provisions of Chapter 183A of the General Laws of Massachusetts, propose to create, and hereby do create with respect to said premises, a condominium to be governed by and subject to the provisions of Chapter 183A, and to that end declare and provide the following:

1. *Name.* The name of the condominium shall be:

(name) CONDOMINIUM

2. *Description of land.* The premises which constitute the condominium consist of _____ square feet of land in Massachusetts at _____, together with the building and improvements thereon. The premises are bounded and described as follows:

Being the same premises conveyed to the Grantors by the following deeds:

3. *Description of buildings.*

4. *Designation of Units and their boundaries.* The Condominium Units and the designations, locations, approximate areas, numbers of rooms, immediately accessible common areas, and other descriptive specifications thereof are as set forth in Exhibit A hereto annexed and on the floor plans also hereto annexed as Exhibit B. The boundaries of each of the Units with respect to the floors, ceilings, and the walls, doors and windows thereof are as follows:

    (a) *Floors:* The upper surface of the subflooring.

    (b) *Ceilings:* The plan of the lower surface of the ceiling joists.

    (c) *Interior Building Walls:* The plane of the surface facing such Unit of the wall studs.

    (d) *Exterior Building Walls, Doors and Windows:* As to walls, the plane of the interior surface of the wall studs; as to doors, the exterior surface thereof; and as to windows, the exterior surfaces of the glass and of the window frames.

5. *Common areas and facilities.* The common areas and facilities of the Condominium consist of:

(a)   The land above described, together with the benefit of, and subject to all rights, easements, restrictions and agreements of record so far as the same may be in force;

(b)   The foundations, structural columns, girders, beams, support, exterior walls, roofs and entrances and exits of the Buildings, and common walls within the Buildings;

(c)   The entrance lobbies, hall and corridors serving more than one Unit and the mailboxes, closets, fire extinguishers and other facilities therein, stairways and fire escapes;

(d)   Installations of central services such as power, light, gas, hot and cold water, including all equipment attendant thereto (but not including equipment contained within and servicing a single Unit);

(e)   All conduits, ducts, plumbing, wiring, flues and other facilities for the furnishing of utility services or waste removal which are contained in portions of the Building contributing to the structure or support thereof, and all such facilities contained within any Unit, which serve parts of the Building other than the Unit within which such facilities are contained, together with an easement of access thereto for maintenance, repair, and replacement, as aforesaid;

(f)   The yards, lawns, gardens, walkways, parking areas and the improvements thereon and thereof, including walls, bulkheads, railings, steps, lighting fixtures and planters; and

(g)   Such additional common areas and facilities as may be defined in Chapter 183A.

The owners of each Unit shall be entitled to an undivided interest in the common areas and facilities in the following percentages set forth opposite each Unit:

UNIT	PERCENTAGE FACTOR	UNIT	PERCENTAGE FACTOR
1	%	13	%
2	%	14	%
3	%	15	%
4	%	16	%
5	%	17	%
6	%	18	%
7	%	19	%
8	%	20	%
9	%	21	%
10	%	22	%
11	%	23	%
12	%	24	%

168

The common areas and facilities shall be subject to the provisions of the By-Laws of *(name)* Condominium Trust hereinafter referred to, and to rules and regulations promulgated pursuant thereto with respect to the use thereof.

6. *Floor plans.* The floor plans of the Buildings showing the layout, location Unit numbers, and dimensions of Units, and bearing the verified statement of a registered architect, registered professional engineer, or registered land surveyor, certifying that the plans fully and accurately depict the same, are attached hereto and captioned *(name)* CONDOMINIUM BUILDINGS AND UNIT PLANS, consisting of *(amount)* sheets, as follows:

7. *Purposes.* The Buildings, and the Units and other facilities therein, are intended to be used only for residential purposes.

The Grantors may, until all of said Units have been sold by said Grantors, (a) lease Units which have not been sold and (b) use any Units owned by the Grantors as models for display for purposes of sale or leasing of Units.

8. *Restrictions on use.* Unless otherwise permitted by instrument in writing duly executed by a majority of the Trustees of said Condominium Trust then in office and pursuant to provisions of the By-Laws thereof:

(a) No Unit shall be used for any purpose other than residential purposes;

(b) The architectural integrity of the Buildings and the Units shall be preserved without modification, and to that end, without limiting the generality of the foregoing, no balcony enclosure, awning, screen, antenna, sign, banner or other device, and no exterior change, addition, structure, projection, decoration or other feature shall be erected or placed upon or attached to any such Unit or any part thereof; no addition to or change or replacement (except, so far as practicable, with identical kind) of any exterior light, door knocker or other exterior hardware, exterior door, or door frames shall be made, and no painting, attaching of decalcomania or other decoration shall be done on any exterior part or surface of any Unit nor on the interior surface of any window, but this subparagraph (b) shall not restrict the right of Unit owners to decorate the interiors of their Units as they may desire; and

(c) No Unit shall be used or maintained in a manner contrary to or inconsistent with the By-Laws of said Condominium Trust and regulations which may be adopted pursuant thereto. Said restrictions shall be for the benefit of the owners of all of the Units, and the Trustees of said Condominium Trust, and shall be enforceable solely by said Unit owners or Trustees, insofar as permitted by law, and shall, insofar as permitted by law; be perpetual; and to that end may be extended at such time or times and in such manner as permitted or required by law for the continued enforeceability thereof. No Unit owner shall be liable for any breach of the provisions of this paragraph except such as occur during his or her ownership thereof.

9.   *Amendments.* This Master Deed may be amended by an instrument in writing (a) signed by the owners of Units entitled to fifty percent (50%) or more of the undivided interests in the common areas and facilities, and (b) signed and acknowledged by a majority of the Trustees of said Condominium Trust and (c) duly recorded with the *(Place)* Registry of Deeds, PROVIDED, HOWEVER, that:

   (a)   The date on which any such instrument is first signed by a Unit owner shall be indicated thereon as the date thereof and no such instrument shall be of any force or effect unless the same has been so recorded within six (6) months after such date;

   (b)   No instrument of amendment which alters the dimensions of any Unit shall be of any force or effect unless the same has been signed by the owner of the Unit so altered;

   (c)   No instrument of amendment which alters the percentage of the undivided interest to which any Unit is entitled in the common areas and facilities shall be of any force or effect unless the same has been signed by the owners of all the Units and said instrument is recorded as an Amended Master Deed;

   (d)   No instrument of amendment affecting any Unit upon which there is a mortgage of record shall be of any force or effect unless the same has been assented to by the holder of such mortgage; and

   (e)   No instrument of amendment which alters this Master Deed in any manner which would render it contrary to or inconsistent with any requirements or provisions of said Chapter 183A of the General Laws of Massachusetts shall be of any force or effect.

10.   *Trust.* The Trust through which the Unit owners will manage and regulate the Condominium established hereby is the Condominium Trust under Declaration of Trust dated   , to be recorded herewith. Said Declaration of Trust establishes a membership organization of which all Unit owners shall be members and in which such owners shall have an interest in proportion to the percentage of undivided interest in the common areas and facilities to which they are entitled hereunder. The names and addresses of the original and present trustees thereof (therein designated as the Trustees thereof) are as follows:

170

1   *(Name and address)*

2   *(Name and address)*

3   *(Name and address)*

Said Trustees have enacted By-Laws, which are set forth in said Declaration of Trust, pursuant to and in accordance with provisions of Chapter 183A of the General Laws of Massachusetts.

11. *Right of First Refusal.* Said Condominium Trust shall have a right of first refusal with respect to all sales of Condominium Units (except the initial sales thereof by the Grantors), and to that end no owner of any Unit shall sell or convey the same to any person unless (1) said owner has received a bona fide offer to purchase the same, (2) said owner has given said Condominium Trust written notice stating the name and address of the offeror and the terms and conditions of said offer and the encumbrances subject to which the Unit is to be conveyed, and containing an offer by said owner to sell said Unit to the trustees of said Condominium Trust on the same terms and conditions as said bona fide offer, and (3) said Trustees of said Condominium Trust shall not within ten (10) days after the giving of such notice have given said owner written notice of the election of said Trustees to purchase said Unit in accordance with said offer. In the event that said Trustees shall so elect to purchase, the deed shall be delivered and the consideration paid at *(Place)* at *(Time)* on the fifteenth (15th) day after the date of the giving of such notice of election to purchase. In the event that said Trustees shall not elect to purchase, then said owner shall be free thereafter to sell and convey said Unit to the offeror named in said owner's notice at a price not lower than that specified therein, but said owner shall not sell or convey said Unit to any other person or at any lower price without again offering the same to said Trustees. The provisions of this paragraph shall not be construed to apply to bona fide mortgagees of any Unit or to sales or other proceedings for the foreclosure thereof. For purposes of this paragraph 11, a lease or tenancy agreement for a term of a year or more shall be deemed to be a sale, and said Condominium Trust shall have a right of first refusal with respect to any such lease, exercisable in the manner aforesaid insofar as applicable. The rights of first refusal hereunder shall not be exercised so as to restrict ownership, use or occupancy of Units because of race, creed, color or national origin. No Unit owner shall be liable for any breach

171

of the provisions of this paragraph except such as occur during his or her ownership thereof.

12.   *Encroachments.* If any portion of the common facilities now encroaches upon any Unit, or if any Unit now encroaches upon any other Unit or upon any portion of the common areas, or if any such encroachment shall occur hereafter as a result of (a) settling of a building, or (b) alteration or repair to the common facilities made by or with the consent of the Trustees, or (c) as a result of repair or restoration of a building or a Unit after damage by fire or other casualty, or (d) as a result of condemnation or eminent domain proceedings, a valid easement shall exist for such encroachment and for the maintenance of the same so long as a building stands.

13.   *Pipes, Wires, Flues, Ducts, Cables, Conduits, Public Utility Lines and other Common Facilities Located Inside of Units.* Each Unit Owner shall have an easement in common with the owners of all other Units to use all pipes, wires, ducts, flues, cables, conduits, public utility lines and other common facilities located in any of the other Units and serving his Unit. Each Unit shall be subject to an easement in favor of the owners of all other Units to use the pipes, wires, ducts, flues, cables, conduits, public utility lines and other common facilities serving such other Units and located in such Unit. The Trustees shall have a right of access to each Unit to inspect the same, to remove violations therefrom and to maintain, repair or replace the common facilities contained therein or elsewhere in the Building.

14.   *Acquisition of Units by Trustees.* In the event (a) any Unit owner shall surrender his Unit, together with: (i) the undivided interest in the common areas and facilities appurtenant thereto; (ii) the interest of such Unit owner in any other Units acquired by the Trustees or their designee on behalf of all Unit owners or the proceeds of the sale or lease thereof, if any; and (iii) the interest of such Unit owner in any other assets of the Condominium; (b) the Trustees shall purchase a Unit from any Unit owner, who has elected to sell same, pursuant to Section 11 hereof; or (c) the Trustees shall purchase a Unit at a foreclosure or other judicial sale, then in any of such events title to any such Unit, together with the appurtenant common areas and facilities, shall be acquired and held by the Trustees or their designee, corporate or otherwise, on behalf of all Unit owners. The lease covering any Unit leased by the Trustees, or their designee, corporate or otherwise, shall be held by the Trustees, or their designee, on behalf of all Unit owners, in proportion to their respective common interests.

15.   *Applicable Law.* The Units and common areas and facilities and the Unit owners and Trustees of said Condominium Trust, shall have

172

the benefit of and be subject to the provisions of Chapter 183A of the General Laws of Massachusetts, and in all respects not specified in this Master Deed or in the Declaration of Trust of said Condominium Trust and the By-Laws set forth therein, shall be governed by provisions of Chapter 183A in their relation to each other and to the Condominium established hereby, including, without limitation, provisions thereof with respect to removal of the Condominium premises or any portion thereof from the provisions of said Chapter 183A.

16. *Definitions.* All terms and expressions herein used which are defined in Section 1 of Chapter 183A shall have the same meanings herein unless the context otherwise requires.

IN WITNESS WHEREOF, on this   day of   , 19__, *(Name)* have signed and sealed this Condominium Master Deed.

_____

_____

_____

THE COMMONWEALTH OF MASSACHUSETTS
ss.   , 19__.

Then personally appeared the above-named *(Name)* and acknowledged the foregoing instrument to be their free act and deed as aforesaid, before me,

_____
NOTARY PUBLIC
My Commission expires:_____

UNIT DEED
of the
(name) CONDOMINIUM

We, *(Name),* recorded with *(Place), (Book____), (Page Number),* as we are the owners of a condominium known as *(Place)* Condominium, created by a Master Deed dated *(Date),* 197 , recorded with *(place)* Registry of Deeds in Book , Page , in accordance with the provisions of G.L.c.183A, GRANT TO _____ with *quitclaim covenants,* the apartment known as Unit __ as referred to in said Master Deed and on the plans registered as part of said Master Deed.

Said Unit contains __ square feet, more or less, and is laid out as shown on a plan recorded herewith, which plan is a copy of a portion of the plans filed with said Master Deed and to which is affixed a verified statement in the form provided for in G.L.c.183A, s.9.

Said Unit is hereby conveyed together with:

1. A __% undivided interest in the common areas and facilities described in said Master Deed. Said Unit has the benefit of the right to use all of said common areas and facilities in common with others entitled thereto as provided in the Declaration of Trust of *(name)* Condominium Trust, the by-laws contained in said Declaration of Trust, and rules and regulations from time to time adopted thereunder, and in particular, but without limitation, to the provisions for assessment of common expenses;

2. An easement for the continuance of all encroachments by the Unit on any adjoining units or common areas existing as a result of construction of the building containing the Unit or which may come into existence hereafter as a result of settling or shifting of such building, or as a result of repair or restoration of such building or of the Unit, after damage or destruction by fire or other casualty, or after taking in condemnation or eminent domain proceedings, or by reason of an alteration or repair to the common areas made by or with the consent of the Trustees;

3. An easement in common with the owners of other units to use any pipes, wires, ducts, flues, cables, conduits, public utility lines and other common facilities located in any of the other units or elsewhere on the condominium property, and serving the Unit.

Said Unit is conveyed subject to:

1. Easements in favor of adjoining units and in favor of the common areas for the continuance of all encroachments of such adjoining units or common areas on the Unit now existing, or which may come into existence hereafter as a result of settling or shifting of the building, or as a result of repair or restoration of the building or of any adjoining unit or of the common areas or facilities after damage or destruction by fire or other casualty, or after

174

taking in condemnation or eminent domain proceedings, or by reason of an alteration or repair to the common areas or facilities made by or with the consent of the Trustees;

2. An easement in favor of the other units to use the pipes, wires, ducts, flues, conduits, cables, public utility lines and other common facilities located in the Unit or elsewhere on the condominium property;

3. The provisions of the Master Deed, By-Laws and floor plans of the Condominium recorded simultaneously with and as part of the Master Deed, as the same may be amended from time to time by instrument recorded in *(place)* Registry of Deeds, which provisions together with any amendments thereto, shall constitute covenants running with the land and shall bind any person having at any time any interest or estate in the Unit, as though such provisions were recited and stipulated at length herein, including without implied limitation the restriction set forth in the Master Deed that said Unit shall be used only for residential purposes (as more particularly described in the Master Deed), and shall not be used for any other purpose, except as may be expressly permitted by the Trustees in accordance with the provisions of said Declaration of Trust.

The grantee acquires said Unit with the benefit of, and subject to the provisions of G.L.c.183A, relating to condominiums, as that statute is written as of the date hereof and as it may in the future be amended.

WITNESS our hands and seals this   day of   197 .

*(name)*_____

*(name)*_____

*(name)*_____

THE COMMONWEALTH OF MASSACHUSETTS

ss. _____, 197 .

Then personally appeared the above named _____ and acknowledged the foregoing to be their free act and deed as aforesaid, before me,

_____

NOTARY PUBLIC

My Commission expires:_____

175

(PROJECT NAME)
CONDOMINIUM TRUST
INDEX

176

(PROJECT NAME)
CONDOMINIUM TRUST

THIS DECLARATION OF TRUST made this ___ day of 197 , at *(place)* and The Commonwealth of Massachusetts by *(Name),* all of said Commonwealth, (hereinafter called the Trustees, which term and any pronoun referring thereto shall be deemed to include their successors in trust hereunder and to mean the trustee or the trustees for the time being hereunder, wherever the context so permits).

ARTICLE I
NAME OF TRUST

The trust hereby created shall be known as *(Name)* CONDOMINIUM TRUST, and under that name, so far as legal, convenient and practicable, shall all business carried on by the Trustees be conducted and shall all instruments in writing by the Trustees be executed.

ARTICLE II
THE TRUST AND ITS PURPOSE

Section 2.1.   General Purposes as per G.L.c.183A

All of the rights and powers in and with respect to the common areas and facilities of the *(Name)* Condominium established by a Master Deed of even date and record herewith which are by virtue of provisions of Chapter 183A of the Massachusetts General Laws conferred upon or exercisable by the organization of unit owners of said Condominium, and all property, real and personal, tangible and intangible, conveyed to the Trustees hereunder shall vest in the Trustees as joint tenants with right of survivorship as trustees of this trust, in trust to exercise, manage, administer and dispose of the same and to receive the income thereof for the benefit of the owners of record from time to time of the units of said Condominium (hereinafter called the Unit Owners), according to the schedule of undivided beneficial interests in the common areas and facilities (hereinafter referred to as the "beneficial interests") set forth in Article IV hereof and in accordance with the provisions of said Chapter 183A, this trust being the organization of the unit owners established pursuant to the provisions of Section 10 of said Chapter 183A for the purposes therein set forth.

Section 2.2.   Trust and Not Partnership

It is hereby expressly declared that a trust and not a partnership has been created and that the Unit Owners are beneficiaries of the Trust, and not partners or associates nor in any other relation whatever between themselves with respect to the trust property, and hold no relation to the Trustees other than that of beneficiaries of the Trust, with only such rights as are conferred

178

upon them as such beneficiaries hereunder and under and pursuant to the provisions of said Chapter 183A of the General Laws.

ARTICLE III

THE TRUSTEES

Section 3.1.   Number of Trustees; Vacancies

There shall at all times be Trustees consisting of such number, not less than two (2) nor more than three (3), as shall be determined from time to time by vote of the Unit Owners entitled to not less than fifty-one (51%) percent of the beneficial interest hereunder. Until *(Name),* own less than three (3) Units, there shall be three (3) Trustees, and they shall be entitled to designate two such Trustees; and until said *(Name),* own less than two (2) Units, they shall be entitled to designate one such Trustee. If and whenever the number of such Trustees shall become less than two (2), a vacancy or vacancies in said office shall be deemed to exist. Each such vacancy shall be filled by instrument in writing setting forth (a) the appointment of a natural person to act as such Trustee, signed (i) by any Unit Owners who certify under oath that Unit Owners entitled to not less than fifty-one percent (51%) of the beneficial interest hereunder, have voted to make such appointment, or (ii) of Unit Owners entitled to such percentage have not within thirty (30) days after the occurrence of any such vacancy made such appointment, by a majority of the then remaining Trustees, or by the sole remaining Trustee if only one, and (b) the acceptance of such appointment, signed and acknowledged by the person so appointed. Such appointment shall become effective upon the recording with *(Place)* Registry of Deeds of a certificate of such appointment signed by a majority of the then remaining Trustees or Trustee if any there be still in office or by said certifying Unit Owners on behalf of Unit Owners holding at least fifty-one percent (51%) of the beneficial interest if there be no such trustees, together with such acceptance, and such person shall then be and become such Trustee and shall be vested with the title to the trust property jointly with the remaining or surviving Trustees or Trustee without the necessity of any act of transfer or conveyance. If for any reason any vacancy in the office of Trustee shall continue for more than sixty (60) days and shall at the end of that time remain unfilled, a Trustee or Trustees to fill such vacancy or vacancies may be appointed by any court of competent jurisdiction upon the application of any Unit Owner or Trustee and notice to all Unit Owners and Trustees and to such other, if any, parties in interest to whom the court may direct that notice be given. The foregoing provisions of this section to the contrary notwithstanding, despite any vacancy in the office of Trustee, however caused and for whatever duration, the remaining or surviving Trustees, subject to the provisions of the immediately following

179

section, shall continue to exercise and discharge all of the powers, discretions and duties hereby conferred or imposed upon the Trustees.

Section 3.2. Action by Majority

In any matters relating to the administration of the trust hereunder and the exercise of the powers hereby conferred, the Trustees may act by majority vote at any duly called meeting at which a quorum is present, as provided in paragraph A of Section 5.10 of Article V; provided, however, that in no event shall a majority consist of less than two (2) Trustees hereunder; and, if and whenever the number of Trustees hereunder shall become less than two (2), the then remaining or surviving Trustees, if any, shall have no power or authority whatsoever to act with respect to the administration of the trust hereunder or to exercise any of the powers hereby conferred except as provided in Section 3.1 of Article III. The Trustees may also act without a meeting by instrument signed by a majority of their number.

Section 3.3. Resignation and Removal of Trustee

Any Trustee may resign at any time by instrument in writing, signed and acknowledged in the manner required in Massachusetts for the acknowledgment of deeds and such resignation shall take effect upon the recording of such instrument with said Registry of Deeds. By vote of Unit Owners entitled to not less than fifty-one percent (51%) of the beneficial interest hereunder, but subject to the right of *(Name)*, recited in Section 3.1 to retain Trustees of their choice, any Trustee may be removed with or without cause, and the vacancy among the Trustees caused by such removal shall be filled in the manner above provided. Such removal shall become effective upon the recording with the said Registry of Deeds of a certificate of removal signed by a majority of the remaining Trustees in office or by three (3) Unit Owners who certify under oath that Unit Owners holding at least fifty-one percent (51%) of the beneficial interest hereunder have voted such removal.

Section 3.4. No Bond by Trustees

No Trustee named or appointed as hereinbefore provided, whether as original Trustee or as successor to or as substitute for another, shall be obliged to give any bond or surety or other security for the performance of any of his duties hereunder, provided, however, that Unit Owners entitled to not less than fifty-one percent (51%) of the beneficial interest hereunder may at any time by instrument in writing signed by them and delivered to the Trustee or Trustees affected require that any one or more of the Trustees shall give bond in such amount and with such sureties as shall be specified in such instrument. All expenses incident to any such bond shall be charged as a common expense of the Condominium.

Section 3.5. Compensation of Trustees

With the approval of a majority of the Trustees, each Trustee may receive such reasonable remuneration for his services and also additional reasonable

180

remuneration for extraordinary or unusual services legal or otherwise, rendered by him in connection with the trusts hereof, all as shall be from time to time fixed and determined by the Trustees, and such remuneration shall be a common expense of the Condominium.

Section 3.6. *No Liability if in Good Faith*

No Trustee hereinbefore named or appointed as hereinbefore provided shall under any circumstances or in any event be held liable or accountable out of his personal assets or be deprived of compensation by reason of any action taken, suffered or omitted in good faith or be so liable or accountable for more money or other property than he actually receives, or for allowing one or more of the other Trustees to have possession of the trust books or property, or be so liable, accountable or deprived by reason of honest errors of judgment or mistakes of fact or law or by reason of the existence of any personal or adverse interest or by reason of anything except his own personal and willful malfeasance and defaults.

Section 3.7. *Self-dealing*

No Trustee shall be disqualified by his office from contracting or dealing with the Trustees or with one or more Unit Owners (whether directly or indirectly because of his interest individually or the Trustees' interest or any Unit Owner's interest in any corporation, hereunder and the exercise of the powers hereby conferred, the Trustee, firm, trust or other organization connected with such contracting or dealing or because of any other reason), as vendor, purchaser or otherwise, nor shall any such dealing, contract or arrangement entered into in respect of this trust in which any Trustee shall be in any way interested be avoided nor shall any Trustee so dealing or contracting or being so interested be liable to account for any profit realized by any such dealing, contract or arrangement by reason of such Trustee's holding office or of the fiduciary relation hereby established, provided the Trustee shall act in good faith and shall disclose the nature of his interest before the dealing, contract or arrangement is entered into.

Section 3.8. *Indemnity*

The Trustees and each of them shall be entitled to indemnity both out of the trust property and by the Unit Owners against any liability incurred by them or any of them in the execution hereof, including without limiting the generality of the foregoing, liabilities in contract and in tort and liabilities for damages, penalties and fines. Each Unit Owner shall be personally liable for all sums lawfully assessed for his share of the common expenses of the Condominium and for his proportionate share of any claims involving the trust property in excess thereof, all as provided in Sections 6 and 13 of said Chapter 183A. Nothing in this paragraph contained shall be deemed, however, to limit in any respect the powers granted to the Trustees in this instrument.

ARTICLE IV
BENEFICIARIES AND THE BENEFICIAL INTEREST IN THE TRUST

Section 4.1. Percentage Interests

The beneficiaries of this trust shall be the Unit Owners of the *(name)* Condominium from time to time. The beneficial interest in the trust hereunder shall be divided among the Unit Owners in the percentages of undivided beneficial interest appertaining to the Units of the Condominium, as follows:

UNIT	PERCENTAGE FACTOR	UNIT	PERCENTAGE FACTOR
1	%	13	%
2	%	14	%
3	%	15	%
4	%	16	%
5	%	17	%
6	%	18	%
7	%	19	%
8	%	20	%
9	%	21	%
10	%	22	%
11	%	23	%
12	%	24	%

Section 4.2. Persons to Vote as Unit Owners

The beneficial interest of each Unit of the Condominium shall be held and exercised as a unit and shall not be divided among several owners of any such Unit. To that end, whenever any of said Units is owned of record by more than one person, the several owners of such Unit shall (a) determine and designate which one of such owners shall be authorized and entitled to cast votes, execute instruments and otherwise exercise the rights appertaining to such Unit hereunder, and (b) notify the Trustees of such designation by a notice in writing signed by all of the record owners of such Unit. Any such designation shall take effect upon receipt by the Trustees and may be changed at any time and from time to time by notice as aforesaid. In the absence of any such notice of designation, the Trustees may designate any one such owner for such purposes.

ARTICLE V
BY-LAWS

The provisions of this Article V shall constitute the By-Laws of this trust and the organization of Unit Owners established hereby, to wit:

Section 5.1. Powers of the Trustees

The Trustees shall, subject to and in accordance with all applicable provi-

182

sions of said Chapter 183A, have the absolute control, management and disposition of the trust property (which term as herein used shall insofar as applicable be deemed to include the common areas and facilities of the Condominium) as if they were the absolute owners thereof, free from the control of the Unit Owners (except as limited in this trust instrument) and, without by the following enumeration limiting the generality of the foregoing or of any item in the enumeration, with full power and uncontrolled discretion, subject only to the limitations and conditions herein and in the provisions of said Chapter 183A, at any time and from time to time and without the necessity of applying to any court or to the Unit Owners for leave so to do:

(i) To retain the trust property, or any part or parts thereof, in the same form or forms of investment in which received or acquired by them so far and so long as they shall think fit, without liability for any loss resulting therefrom;

(ii) To sell, assign, convey, transfer, exchange, and otherwise deal with or dispose of, the trust property, but not the whole thereof, free and discharged of any and all trusts, at public or private sale, to any person or persons, for cash or on credit, and in such manner, on such restrictions, stipulations, agreements and reservations as they shall deem proper, including the power to take back mortgages to secure the whole or any part of the purchase price of any of the trust property sold or transferred by them, and to execute and deliver any deed or other instrument in connection with the foregoing;

(iii) To purchase or otherwise acquire title to, and to rent, lease or hire from others for terms which may extend beyond the termination of this trust any property or rights to property, real or personal, and to own, manage, use and hold such property and such rights;

(iv) To borrow or in any other manner raise such sum or sums of money or other property as they shall deem advisable in any manner and on any terms, and to evidence the same by notes, bonds, securities or other evidences of indebtedness, which may mature at a time or times, even beyond the possible duration of this trust, and to execute and deliver any mortgage, pledge or other instrument to secure any such borrowing;

(v) To enter into any arrangement for the use or occupation of the trust property, or any part or parts thereof, including, without thereby limiting the generality of the foregoing, leases, subleases, easements, licenses or concessions, upon such terms and conditions and with such stipulations and agreements as they shall deem desirable, even if the same extend beyond the possible duration of this trust;

(vi) To invest and reinvest the trust property, or any parts thereof and from time to time and as often as they shall see fit to change investments, including power to invest in all types of securities and other property, of whatsoever nature and however denominated, all to such extent as to them shall seem proper, and without liability for loss, even though such property or such investments shall be of a character or in an amount not customarily considered proper for the investment of trust funds or which does or may not produce income;

(vii)   To incur such liabilities, obligations and expenses, and to pay from the principal or the income of the trust property in their hands all such sums as they shall deem necessary or proper for the furtherance of the purposes of the trust;

(viii)   To determine whether receipt by them constitutes principal or income or surplus and to allocate between principal and income and to designate as capital or surplus any of the funds of the trust;

(ix)   To vote in such manner as they shall think fit any or all shares in any corporation or trust which shall be held as trust property, and for that purpose to give proxies, to any person or persons or to one or more of their number, to vote, waive any notice or otherwise act in respect of any such shares;

(x)   To deposit any funds of the trust in any bank or trust company, and to delegate to any one or more of their number, or to any other person or persons, the power to deposit, withdraw and draw checks on any funds of the trust;

(xi)   To maintain such offices and other places of business as they shall deem necessary or proper and to engage in business in Massachusetts or elsewhere;

(xii)   To employ, appoint and remove such agents, managers, officers, board of managers, brokers, engineers, architects, employees, servants, assistants and counsel (which counsel may be a firm of which one or more of the Trustees are members) as they shall deem proper for the purchase, sale or management of the trust property, or any part or parts thereof, or for conducting the business of the trust, and may define their respective duties and fix and pay their compensation, and the Trustees shall not be answerable for the acts and defaults of any such person. The Trustees may delegate to any such agent, manager, officer, board, broker, engineer, architect, employee, servant, assistant or counsel any or all of their powers (including discretionary powers, except that the power to join in amending, altering, adding to, terminating or changing this Declaration of Trust and the trust hereby created shall not be delegated) all for such times and purposes as they shall deem proper. Without hereby limiting the generality of the foregoing, the Trustees may designate from their number a Chairman, a Treasurer, a Secretary, and such other officers as they deem fit, and may from time to time designate one or more of their own number to be the Managing Trustee or Managing Trustees, for the

184

management and administration of the trust property and the business of the trust, or any part or parts thereof;

(xiii)   Generally, in all matters not herein otherwise specified, to control, do each and every thing necessary, suitable, convenient, or proper for the accomplishment of any of the purposes of the trust or incidental to the powers herein or in said Chapter 183A, manage and dispose of the trust property as if the Trustees were the absolute owners thereof and to do any and all acts, including the execution of any instruments, which by their performance thereof shall be shown to be in their judgment for the best interests of the Unit Owners.

Section 5.2.   Maintenance and Repair of Units

The Unit Owners shall be responsible for the proper maintenance and repair of their respective Units and the maintenance, repair and replacement of utility fixtures therein serving the same, including, without limitation, interior finish walls, ceilings, and floors; the interior portions of windows and window frames, and interior window trim; doors; the interior portions of door frames and interior door trim; plumbing and sanitary waste fixtures and fixtures for water and other utilities; electrical fixtures and outlets; and all wires, pipes, drains and conduits for water, sewerage, electric power and light, telephone and any other utility services which are contained in and serve such Unit. If the Trustees shall at any time in their reasonable judgment determine that the interior of a Unit is in such need of maintenance or repair that the market value of one or more other Units is being adversely affected or that the condition of a Unit or any fixtures, furnishing, facility or equipment therein is hazardous to any unit or the occupants thereof, the Trustees shall in writing request the Unit Owner to perform the needed maintenance, repair or replacement or to correct the hazardous condition, and in case such work shall not have been commenced within fifteen days (or such reasonable shorter period in case of emergency as the Trustees shall determine) of such request and thereafter diligently brought to completion, the Trustees shall be entitled to have the work performed for the account of such Unit Owner whose Unit is in need of work and to enter upon and have access to such Unit for the purpose, and the cost of such work as is reasonably necessary therefor shall constitute a lien upon such Unit and the Unit Owner thereof shall be personally liable therefor.

Section 5.3.   Maintenance, Repair and Replacement of Common Areas and Facilities and Assessment of Common Expenses Thereof

The Trustees shall be responsible for the proper maintenance, repair and replacement of the common areas and facilities of the Condominium (see Section 5.5 for specific provisions dealing with repairs and replacement necessitated because of casualty loss) and such may be done through the Managing

185

Agent, as hereinafter provided, and any two trustees or the Managing Agent, or any others who may be so designated by the Trustees, may approve payment of vouchers for such work, and the expenses of such maintenance, repair and replacement shall be assessed to the Unit Owners as common expenses of the Condominium at such times and in such amounts as provided in Section 5.4.

Section 5.4. *Common Expenses, Profits and Funds*

A. The Unit Owners shall be liable for common expenses and entitled to common profits of the Condominium in proportion to their respective percentages of beneficial interest as determined in Article IV hereof. The Trustees may at any time or times distribute common profits among the Unit Owners in such proportions. The Trustees may, to such extent as they deem advisable, set aside common funds of the Condominium as reserve or contingent funds, and may use the funds so set aside for reduction of indebtedness or other lawful capital purpose, or subject to the provisions of the following paragraphs B and C of this Section 5.4, for repair, rebuilding or restoration of the trust property or for improvements thereto, and the funds so set aside shall not be deemed to be common profits available for distribution.

B. At least thirty (30) days prior to the commencement of each fiscal year of this trust the Trustees shall estimate the common expenses expected to be incurred during such fiscal year together with a reasonable provision for contingencies and reserves, and after taking into account any undistributed common profits from prior years, shall determine the assessment to be made for such fiscal year. The Trustees shall promptly render statements to the Unit Owners for their respective shares of such assessment, according to their percentages of interest in the common areas and facilities, and such statements shall, unless otherwise provided therein, be due and payable within thirty (30) days after the same are rendered. In the event that the Trustees shall determine during any fiscal year that the assessment so made is less than the common expenses actually incurred, or in the reasonable opinion of the Trustees likely to be incurred, the Trustees shall make a supplemental assessment or assessments and render statements therefor in the manner aforesaid, and such statements shall be payable and take effect as aforesaid. The Trustees may in their discretion provide for payments of statements in monthly or other installments. The amount of each such statement shall be a personal liability of the Unit Owner and if not paid when due shall carry a late charge at a rate equal to the *(name of bank)* prime interest rate at the time such payment was due and shall constitute a lien on the Unit of the Unit Owner assessed, pursuant to provisions of Section 6 of said Chapter 183A.

C. No Unit Owner shall file an application for abatement of real estate taxes without the approval of the Trustees.

D. The Trustees shall expend common funds only for common expenses

186

and lawful purposes permitted hereby and by provisions of said Chapter 183A.

Section 5.5. Rebuilding and Restoration, Improvements

A.   In the event of any casualty loss to the trust property the Trustees shall determine in their reasonable discretion whether or not such loss exceeds ten percent (10%) of the value of the Condominium immediately prior to the casualty, and shall notify all Unit Owners of such determination. If such loss as so determined does not exceed ten percent (10%) of such value, the Trustees shall proceed with the necessary repairs, rebuilding or restoration in the manner provided in paragraph (a) of Section 17 of said Chapter 183A. If such loss as so determined does exceed ten percent (10%) of such value, the Trustees shall forthwith submit to all Unit Owners (a) a form of agreement (which may be in several counterparts) by the Unit Owners authorizing the Trustees to proceed with the necessary repair, rebuilding or restoration, and (b) a copy of the provision of said Section 17; and the Trustees shall thereafter proceed in accordance with, and take such further action as they may in their discretion deem advisable in order to implement the provisions of paragraph (b) of said Section 17.

B.   If and whenever the Trustees shall propose to make any improvement to the common areas and facilities of the Condominium, or shall be requested in writing by the Unit Owners holding twenty-five percent (25%) or more of the beneficial interest in this trust to make any such improvement, the Trustees shall submit to all Unit Owners (a) a form of agreement (which may be in several counterparts) specifying the improvement or improvements proposed to be made and the estimated cost thereof, and authorizing the Trustees to proceed to make the same, and (b) a copy of the provisions of Section 18 of said Chapter 183A. Upon (a) the receipt by the Trustees of such agreement signed by the Unit Owners holding seventy-five percent (75%) or more of the beneficial interest or (b) the expiration of ninety (90) days after such agreement was first submitted to the Unit Owners, whichever of said (a) and (b) shall first occur, the trustees shall notify all Unit Owners of the aggregate percentage of beneficial interest held by Unit Owners who have then signed such agreement. If such percentage exceeds seventy-five percent (75%), the Trustees shall proceed to make the improvement or improvements specified in such agreement and, in accordance with said Section 18 of Chapter 183A, shall charge the cost of improvement to all the Unit Owners. The agreement so circulated may also provide for separate agreement by the Unit Owners that if Unit Owners holding more than fifty percent (50%) but less than seventy-five percent (75%) of the beneficial interest so consent, the Trustees shall proceed to make such improvement or improvements and shall charge the same to the Unit Owners so consenting.

C.   Notwithstanding anything in the preceding paragraphs A and B contained, (a) in the event that any Unit Owner or Owners shall by notice in writing to the Trustees dissent from any determination of the Trustees with respect to the value of the Condominium or any other determination or action of the Trustees under this Section 5.5, and such dispute shall not be resolved within thirty (30) days after such notice, then either the Trustees or the dissenting Unit Owner or Owners may submit the matter to arbitration, and for that purpose one arbitrator shall be designated by the Trustees, one by the dissenting Unit Owner or Owners and a third by the two arbitrators so designated, and such arbitration shall be conducted in accordance with the rules and procedures of the American Arbitration Association, and (b) the Trustees shall not in any event be obliged to proceed with any repair, rebuilding or restoration, or any improvement, unless and until they have received funds in an amount equal to the estimate of the Trustees of all costs thereof.

Section 5.6.   Rules, Regulations, Restrictions and Requirements

The Trustees may at any time and from time to time adopt, amend and rescind administrative rules and regulations governing the details of the operation and use of the common areas and facilities, and such restrictions on and requirements respecting the use and maintenance of the Units and the use of the common areas and facilities as are consistent with provisions of the Master Deed and are designed to prevent unreasonable interference with the use by the Unit Owners of their Units and of the common areas and facilities.

Section 5.7.   Managing Agent

The Trustees may, at their discretion, appoint a manager or managing agent to administer the Condominium, who shall perform such duties in the administration, management and operation of the Condominium, including the incurring of expenses, the making of disbursements and the keeping of accounts, as the Trustees shall from time to time determine. The Trustees or such manager or managing agent may appoint, employ and remove such additional agents, attorneys, accountants or employees as the Trustees may from time to time determine.

Section 5.8.   Insurance

The Trustees shall obtain and maintain, to the extent available, master policies of insurance of the following kinds, naming the Trust, the Trustees, all of the Unit Owners and their mortgagees as insureds as their interests appear:

A.   Casualty or physical damage insurance on the Building and all other insurable improvements forming part of the Condominium (including all of the Units but not including the furniture, furnishings and other personal property of the Unit Owners therein), together with the service machinery, apparatus, equipment and installations located in the Condominium, and existing for the provision of central services or for common use, in an amount not less than eighty percent (80%) of their full replacement value (exclusive of foundations) as determined by the Trustees in their judgment, against (1) loss or damage by fire and other hazards covered by the standard extended coverage endorsement, together with coverage for the payment of common expenses with respect to damaged Units during the period of reconstruction, and (2) such other hazards and risks as the Trustees from time to time in their discretion shall determine to be appropriate, including but not limited to vandalism, malicious mischief, windstorm and water damage, boiler and machinery explosion or damage and plate glass damage. All policies of casualty or physical damage insurance shall provide (1) that such policies may not be cancelled or substantially modified without at least ten (10) days' prior written notice to all of the insureds, including each Unit mortgagee and (2) that the coverage thereof shall not be terminated for nonpayment of premiums without thirty (30) days' notice to all of the insureds including each Unit mortgagee. Certificates of such insurance and all renewals thereof, together with proof of payment of premiums, shall be delivered by the Trustees to all Unit Owners and their mortgagees upon request, at least ten (10) days prior to the expiration of the then current policies.

B.   Comprehensive public liability insurance in such amounts and forms as shall be determined by the Trustees, covering the Trust, the Trustees, all of the Unit Owners and any manager or managing agent of the Condominium, and with cross liability endorsement to cover liability of any insured to other insureds.

C.   Workmen's compensation and employer's liability insurance covering any employees of the Trust.

D.   Such other insurance as the Trustees shall determine to be appropriate.

Such master policies shall provide that all casualty loss proceeds thereunder shall be paid to the Trustees as insurance trustees under these by-laws. The sole duty of the Trustees as such insurance trustees shall be to receive such proceeds as are paid and to hold, use and disburse the same for the purposes stated in this Section and Section 5.5. If repair or restoration of the damaged portions of the Condominium is to be made, all insurance loss proceeds shall be held in shares for the Trust and the owners of damaged Units in proportion to the respective costs of repair or restoration of the damaged portions of the common areas and facilities of each damaged Unit, with each share to be disbursed to defray the respective costs of repair or restoration of the damaged common areas and facilities and damaged Units, and with any excess of any such share of proceeds above such costs of repair

189

or restoration to be paid to the Trust or Unit Owner for whom held upon completion of repair or restoration; but if pursuant to Section 5.5, restoration or repair is not to be made, all insurance loss proceeds shall be held as common funds of the Trust and applied for the benefit of Unit Owners in proportion to their percentage interests as listed in Section 4.1 if the Condominium is totally destroyed, and, in the event of a partial destruction, to those Unit Owners who have suffered damage in proportion to the damage suffered by them. Such application for the benefit of Unit Owners shall include payment directly to a Unit Owner's mortgagee if the mortgage with respect to such unit so requires. Such master policies shall contain (1) waivers of subrogation as to any claims against the Trust, the Trustees and their agents and employees, and against the Unit Owners and their respective employees, agents and guests, (2) waivers of any defense based on the conduct of any insured, and (3) provisions to the effect that the insurer shall not be entitled to contribution as against casualty insurance which may be purchased by individual Unit Owners as hereinafter permitted.

Each Unit Owner or his mortgagee may obtain additional insurance at his own expense, provided that all such insurance shall contain provisions similar to those required to be contained in the Trust's master policies waiving the insurer's rights to subrogation and contribution. If the proceeds from the master policies on account of any casualty loss are reduced due to proration with insurance individually purchased by a Unit Owner, such Unit Owner agrees to assign the proceeds of such individual insurance, to the extent of the amount of such reduction, to the Trustees to be distributed as herein provided. Each Unit Owner shall promptly notify the Trustees of all improvements made by him to his Unit, the value of which exceeds One Thousand ($1,000.00) Dollars, and such Unit Owner shall pay to the Trustees as an addition to his share of the common expenses of the Condominium otherwise payable by him any increase in insurance premium incurred by the Trust which results from such improvement.

E. The cost of such insurance shall be deemed a common expense assessable and payable as provided in Section 5.4.

Section 5.9.   Right of First Refusal

The right of first refusal with respect to sales of Units as set forth in the Master Deed shall be exercised by the Board of Trustees. In the event that the Trustees shall elect to purchase or lease a Unit pursuant to the provisions thereof, the purchase price, or rent, and other costs in connection therewith shall constitute common expenses and the Trustees may expend common funds therefor.

190

Section 5.10. Meetings

A. The Trustees shall meet annually on the date of the annual meeting of the Unit Owners and at such meeting may elect the Chairman, Treasurer, Secretary and any other officers they deem expedient. Other meetings may be called by any Trustee and in such other manner as the Trustees may establish, provided, however, that written notice of each meeting stating the place, day and hour thereof shall be given at least two days before such meeting to each Trustee. A majority of the number of Trustees then in office shall constitute a quorum at all meetings, and such meetings shall be conducted in accordance with such rules as the Trustees may adopt.

B. There shall be an annual meeting of the Unit Owners on the third Wednesday in January in each year at 8:00 P.M. at such reasonable place and time as may be designated by the Trustees by written notice given to the Unit Owners at least seven days prior to the date so designated. Special meetings (including a meeting in lieu of a passed annual meeting) of the Unit Owners may be called at any time by the Trustees and shall be called by them upon the written request of any Unit Owner. Written notice of any such meeting designating the place, day and hour thereof shall be given by the Trustees to the Unit Owners at least seven (7) days prior to the date so designated.

Section 5.11. Notices to Unit Owners

Every notice to any Unit Owner required under the provisions hereof, or which may be deemed by the Trustees necessary or desirable in connection with the execution of the trust created hereby or which may be ordered in any judicial proceeding shall be deemed sufficient and binding if a written or printed copy of such notice shall be given by one or more of the Trustees to such Unit Owner by mailing it, postage prepaid, and addressed to such Unit Owner at his address as it appears upon the records of the Trustees or by delivery or mailing the same to such Unit or, if no address appears, in any case, at least seven (7) days prior to the date fixed for the happening of the matter, thing or event of which such notice is given.

Section 5.12. Inspection of Books; Reports to Unit Owners

Books, accounts and records of the Trustees shall be open to inspection to any one or more of the Trustees and the Unit Owners at all reasonable times. The Trustees shall, as soon as reasonably possible after the close of each fiscal year, or oftener if convenient to them, submit to the Unit Owners a report of the operations of the Trustees for such year which shall include financial statements certified by a certified public accountant in such summary from and in only such detail as the Trustees shall deem proper. Any person who has been furnished with such report and shall have failed to object thereto by notice in writing to the Trustees given by registered mail within a period of one month of the date of the receipt by him shall be deemed to have assented thereto.

191

Section 5.13. Checks, Notes, Drafts, and Other Instruments

Checks, notes, drafts and other instruments for the payment of money drawn or endorsed in the names of the Trustees or of the trust may be signed by any two Trustees (or by one Trustee if there is only one), or by any person or persons to whom such power may at any time or from time to time be delegated by not less than a majority of the Trustees.

Section 5.14. Seal

The seal of the Trustees shall be circular in form, bearing the inscription *(name of condominium trust)* - but such seal may be altered by the Trustees at pleasure, and the Trustees may, at any time or from time to time, at their option, adopt a common or wafer seal which shall be valid for all purposes, or they may sign any instrument under seal without being required to affix a formal, common or wafer seal.

Section 5.15. Fiscal Year

The fiscal year of the trust shall be the year ending with the last day of December or such other date as may from time to time be determined by the Trustees.

ARTICLE VI
RIGHTS AND OBLIGATIONS OF THIRD PARTIES
DEALING WITH THE TRUSTEES

Section 6.1. Reliance of Third Parties

No purchaser, mortgagee, lender or other person dealing with the Trustees as they then appear of record in said Registry of Deeds shall be bound to ascertain or inquire further as to the persons who are then Trustees hereunder, or be affected by any notice, implied or actual, otherwise than by a certificate thereof, and such record or certificate shall be conclusive evidence of the personnel of said Trustees and of any changes therein. The receipts of the Trustees, or any one or more of them, for moneys or things paid or delivered to them or him shall be effectual discharges therefrom to the persons paying or delivering the same and no person from whom the Trustees, or any one or more of them, shall receive any money, property or other credit shall be required to see to the application thereof. No purchaser, mortgagee, lender or other person dealing with the Trustees or with any real or personal property which then is or formerly was trust property shall be bound to ascertain or inquire as to the existence or occurrence of any event or purpose in or for which a sale, mortgage, pledge or charge is herein authorized or directed, or otherwise as to the purpose or regularity of any of the acts of the Trustees, or any one or more of them, purporting to be done in pursuance of any of the provisions or powers herein contained, or as to the regularity of the

192

resignation or appointment of any Trustee, and any instrument of appointment of a new Trustee or resignation of an old Trustee purporting to be executed by the Trustees, Unit Owners or other persons herein required to execute the same, shall be conclusive evidence in favor of any such purchaser or other person dealing with the Trustees of the matters therein recited relating to such discharge, resignation or appointment or the occasion thereof.

Section 6.2. No Recourse against Trustees

No recourse shall at any time be had under or upon any note, bond, contract, order, instrument, certificate, undertaking, obligation, covenant, or agreement, whether oral or written, made, issued, or executed by the Trustees or by any agent or employee of the Trustees, or by reason of anything done or omitted to be done by or on behalf of them or any of them, against the Trustees individually, or against any such agent or employee, or against any beneficiary, either directly or indirectly, by legal or equitable proceedings, or by virtue of any suit or otherwise, and all persons extending credit to, contracting with or having any claim against the Trustees, shall look only to the trust property for payment under such contract or claim, or for the payment of any debt, damage, judgment or decree, or of any money that may otherwise become due or payable to them from the Trustees, so that neither the Trustees nor the beneficiaries, present or future, shall be personally liable therefor; provided, however, that nothing herein contained shall be deemed to limit or impair the liability of Unit Owners under provisions of Section 8 of Article III hereof or under provisions of said Chapter 183A.

Section 6.3. Instruments Subject to Trust Terms

Every note, bond, contract, order, instrument, certificate, undertaking, obligation, covenant or agreement, whether oral or written, made, issued or executed by the Trustees, or by any agent or employee of the Trustees, shall be deemed to have been entered into subject to the terms, conditions, provisions and restrictions hereof, whether or not express reference shall have been made to this instrument.

Section 6.4. Certificates by Trustees

This Declaration of Trust and any amendments hereto and any certificate herein required to be recorded and any other certificate or paper signed by said Trustees or any of them which it may be deemed desirable to record shall be recorded with said Registry of Deeds and such record shall be deemed conclusive evidence of the contents and effectiveness thereof according to the tenor thereof; and all persons dealing in any manner whatsoever with the Trustees, the trust property or any beneficiary thereunder shall be held to have notice of any alteration or amendment of this Declaration of Trust, or change of Trustee or Trustees, when the same shall be recorded with said Registry of Deeds. Any certificate signed by two Trustees in office at the time (only one Trustee if there is only one at the time), setting forth as facts any matters affecting the trust, including statements as to who are the beneficiaries, as to what action has been taken by the beneficiaries, and as to matters determining the authority of the Trustees to do any act, when duly acknowledged and recorded with said Registry of Deeds shall be conclusive evidence as to the existence of such alleged facts in favor of all third persons, including the Trustees, acting in reliance thereon. Any certificate executed by any Trustee hereunder, or by a majority of the Trustees hereunder, setting forth the existence of any facts, the existence of which is necessary to authorize the execution of any instrument or the taking of any action by such Trustee or majority, as the case may be, shall, as to all persons acting in good faith in reliance thereon be conclusive evidence of the truth of the statements made in such certificate and of the existence of the facts therein set forth.

ARTICLE VII

AMENDMENTS AND TERMINATION

Section 7.1.   Amendment of Trust

The Trustees, with the consent in writing of Unit Owners entitled to not less than sixty-five percent (65%) of the beneficial interest hereunder, may at any time and from time to time amend, alter, add to, or change this Declaration of Trust in any manner or to any extent, the Trustees first, however, being duly indemnified to their reasonable satisfaction against outstanding obligations and liabilities; provided always, however, that no such amendment, alteration, addition or change (a) according to the purport of which the percentage of the beneficial interest hereunder of any Unit Owner would be altered or in any manner or to any extent whatsoever modified or affected, so as to be different from the percentage of the individual interest of such Unit Owner in the common areas and facilities as set forth in the Master Deed, or (b) which would render this trust contrary to or inconsistent with any requirements or provisions of said Chapter 183A, shall be valid or effective. Any amendment, alteration, addition or change pursuant to the foregoing provisions of this paragraph shall become effective upon the recording with said Registry of Deeds of an instrument of amendment, alteration, addition or change, as the case may be, signed, sealed and acknowledged in the manner required in Massachusetts for the acknowledgment of deeds, by any two Trustees, if there be at least two then in office (or one Trustee if there be only one), setting forth in full the amendment, alteration, addition or change and reciting the consent of the Unit Owners herein required to consent thereto.

194

Such instrument, so executed and recorded, shall be conclusive evidence of the existence of all facts and of compliance with all prerequisites to the validity of such amendment, alteration, addition or change, whether stated in such instrument or not, upon all questions as to title or affecting the rights of third persons and for all other purposes. Nothing in this paragraph contained shall be construed as making it obligatory upon the Trustees to amend, alter, add or to change the Declaration of Trust upon obtaining the necessary consent as hereinbefore provided.

Section 7.2. *Termination*

The trust hereby created shall terminate only upon the removal of the *(Name)* Condominium from the provisions of said Chapter 183A in accordance with the procedure therefor set forth in Section 19 of said Chapter.

Section 7.3. *Disposition of Property on Termination*

Upon the termination of this trust, the Trustees may, subject to and in accordance with the provisions of said Chapter 183A, sell and convert into money the whole of the trust property, or any part or parts thereof, and, after paying or retiring all known liabilities and obligations of the Trustees and providing for indemnity against any other outstanding liabilities and obligations, shall divide the proceeds thereof among, and distribute in kind, at valuations made by them which shall be conclusive, all other property then held by them in trust hereunder, to the Unit Owners according to their respective percentages of beneficial interest hereunder. And in making any sale under this provision the Trustees shall have power to sell by public auction or private contract and to buy in or rescind or vary any contract of sale and to resell without being answerable for loss and, for said purposes, to do all things, including the execution and delivery of instruments, as may by their performance thereof be shown to be in their judgment necessary or desirable in connection therewith. The powers of sale and all other powers herein given to the Trustees shall continue as to all property at any time remaining in their hands or ownership, even though all times herein fixed for distribution of trust property may have passed.

ARTICLE VIII

CONSTRUCTION AND INTERPRETATION

In the construction hereof, whether or not so expressed, words used in the singular or in the plural respectively include both the plural and singular, words denoting males include females and words denoting persons include individuals, firms, associations, companies (joint stock or otherwise), trusts and corporations unless a contrary intention is to be inferred from or required by the subject matter or context. The cover, title, headings of different parts

195

hereof, the table of contents and the marginal notes, if any, are inserted only for convenience of reference and are not to be taken to be any part hereof or to control or affect the meaning, construction, interpretation or effect hereof. All the trusts, powers and provisions herein contained shall take effect and be construed according to the laws of the Commonwealth of Massachusetts. Unless the context otherwise indicates, words defined in said Chapter 183A shall have the same meaning herein.

IN WITNESS WHEREOF said have hereunto set their hands and seals on the day and year first hereinabove set forth.

_____

(Name)

_____

(Name)

_____

(Name)

THE COMMONWEALTH OF MASSACHUSETTS
ss._____, 197 .

Then personally appeared the above-named (Name) and acknowledged the foregoing instrument to be their free act and deed, before me,

_____

NOTARY PUBLIC
My Commission expires:_____

Appendix D

FEDERAL REGULATORY REQUIREMENTS

Today, condominium developments are being regulated on a federal level as well as on a state level. Such federal regulations apply mainly to rental resort condominium developments that are being offered as an investment due to the income potential from a rental pool. Developers of such offerings are required to register their business with the Security Exchange Commission, which requires that a prospectus be submitted that offers a full disclosure of the offering plan. Such a prospectus must be made available to the prospective purchasers before purchase and sale agreements may be signed. It is most important that such a report be thoroughly understood by the investor, as there are many risks in the rental business. If the developer of a rental pool condominium development has not registered his business with the Security Exchange Commission, one should stay clear of the development, for the Security Exchange Commission can require registration at any time which can cause damaging delays.

Appendix E

DEPRECIATION CALCULATIONS

Each year, one may deduct, as depreciation, a reasonable figure for the wear and tear of one's business or income producing property, until one's costs have been recovered during the property's useful life. Consequently, depreciation deductions are allowable for commercial and rental resort condominiums but not for residential condominiums unless rented out.

Although there are various methods for computing depreciation, the two methods that are most commonly used are:

1) Straight line
2) Declining balance

The Straight Line method of depreciation is the simplest method

197

to compute and is generally used by persons planning to hold their property for more than a few years. The Declining Balance method of depreciation, on the other hand, is most often used by persons not planning to hold their property for more than a few years, for one can depreciate a larger portion of the property in the first few years. Both methods are further explained in the following presentations.

Straight line depreciation

Under the straight line method, one deducts the cost of the building structure in equal amounts over the period of the building's estimated useful life. Shown below is an example of the straight line method of computation. It will be assumed that the structure to be depreciated is the $35,000 commercial condominium.

Commercial Condominium - $35,000
Land Value - 5,000
Building Value - 30,000
Useful Life - 35 years
Rate of Depreciation/year = 1/Number of Years
= 1/35 = 2.85%

Year	Value	×	Rate	=	Depreciation Deduction
1st year	$30,000	×	2.85%	=	$860
2nd year	$30,000	×	2.85%	=	$860
3rd year	$30,000	×	2.85%	=	$860
10th year	$30,000	×	2.85%	=	$860
20th year	$30,000	×	2.85%	=	$860
35th year	$30,000	×	2.85%	=	$860

Declining Balance Depreciation

Under the declining balance method, each year's depreciation is subtracted from the value of the property before computing the following year's depreciation. Consequently the depreciation rate applies to a smaller value each succeeding year, resulting in a smaller deduction each succeeding year. But one may use a rate that is 1½ or 2 times as great as the rate used for the straight line method if purchasing *new* year-round rental property.

Shown below is an example of the declining balance method that is 1½ times the straight line rate. Because the rental resort condominium in the previous text was purchased as a short term investment, a declining balance computation of depreciation was used in the cost sheet as calculated below:

Resort Condominium		-$35,000
Land Value		-$ 5,000
Building Value		-$30,000
Useful Life		-30 years

Straight Line Depreciation Rate/Year = 1/number of years
   = 1/30 = 3.33%
Declining Balance Rate/Year = 3.33% × 1.5 = 5.0%

Year	Value	×	Rate	=	Depreciation Deduction
1st Year	$30,000	×	5.0%	=	$1,500
2nd Year	$28,500	×	5.0%	=	$1,425
3rd Year	$27,075	×	5.0%	=	$1,354
——					
10th Year	$18,907	×	5.0%	=	$ 945
——					
20th Year	$11,320	×	5.0%	=	$ 566
30th Year	$ 6,780	×	5.0%	=	$ 339

It should be noted that the $1,204 figure used in the resort condominium example in the text was the average depreciation deduction over the first 10 years. Such an average figure assumes a 10 year investment cycle.

In summary, it should be made clear that the figures shown in the above examples are only for the use of explanation and should not be viewed as fact. For instance, the useful life can vary from 10 to 50 years depending on the material used in the structure of the building. Because the techniques used for computing depreciation are constantly being updated, it is highly recommended that one consult his tax accountant or the IRS before computing such depreciation on his tax returns.

Appendix F

Mortgage Payment Table*
7½% - 20 Years

Mortgage Amount	Total Monthly Cost	Yearly Cost	Principal/Yr. (Averaged over 1st Ten Years)	Interest/Yr.
$15,000	$120.84	$1,450.08	$ 481.50	$ 968.58
17,500	140.98	1,691.76	568.75	1,123.01
20,000	161.12	1,933.44	642.00	1,291.44
22,500	181.26	2,175.12	722.25	1,452.87
25,000	201.40	2,416.80	802.50	1,614.30
27,500	221.54	2,658.48	882.75	1,775.73
30,000	241.68	2,900.16	963.00	1,937.16
35,000	281.96	3,383.52	1,123.50	2,260.02
40,000	322.24	3,866.88	1,284.00	2,582.88
45,000	362.52	4,350.24	1,444.50	2,905.74
50,000	402.80	4,833.60	1,605.00	3,228.60
55,000	443.08	5,316.96	1,765.50	3,551.46
60,000	483.36	5,800.32	1,926.00	3,874.32

Mortgage Payment Table*
7½% - 25 Years

Mortgage Amount	Total Monthly Cost	Yearly Cost	Principal/Yr. (Averaged over 1st Ten Years)	Interest/Yr.
$15,000	$110.85	$1,330.20	$ 304.50	$1,025.70
17,500	129.33	1,551.96	355.25	1,196.71
20,000	147.80	1,773.60	406.00	1,367.60
22,500	166.28	1,995.36	456.75	1,538.61
25,000	184.75	2,217.00	507.50	1,709.50
27,500	203.23	2,438.76	558.25	1,880.51
30,000	221.70	2,660.40	609.00	2,051.40
35,000	258.65	3,103.80	710.50	2,393.30
40,000	295.60	3,547.20	812.00	2,735.20
45,000	332.55	3,990.60	913.50	3,077.10
50,000	369.50	4,434.00	1,015.00	3,419.00
55,000	406.45	4,877.40	1,116.50	3,760.09
60,000	443.40	5,320.80	1,218.00	4,102.80

*Approximate

Mortgage Payment Table*
8% - 20 Years

Mortgage Amount	Total Monthly Cost	Yearly Cost	Principal/Yr. (Averaged over 1st Ten Years)	Interest/Yr.
$15,000	$125.47	$1,505.64	$ 466.50	$1,039.14
17,500	146.38	1,756.56	544.25	1,212.31
20,000	167.29	2,007.48	622.00	1,385.48
22,500	188.20	2,258.40	699.75	1,558.65
25,000	209.12	2,509.44	777.50	1,731.94
27,500	230.03	2,760.36	855.25	1,905.11
30,000	250.94	3,011.28	933.00	2,078.28
35,000	292.76	3,513.12	1,088.50	2,424.62
40,000	334.58	4.014.96	1,244.00	2,770.96
45,000	376.40	4,516.80	1,399.50	3,117.30
50,000	418.23	5,018.76	1,555.00	3,463.76
55,000	460.05	5,520.60	1,710.50	3,810.10
60,000	501.87	6,022.44	1,866.00	4,156.44

Mortgage Payment Table*
8%–25 years

Mortgage Amount	Total Monthly Cost	Yearly Cost	Principal/Yr. (Averaged over 1st Ten Years)	Interest/Yr.
$15,000	$115.78	$1,389.36	$ 288.00	$1,101.36
17,500	135.07	1,620.84	336.00	1,284.84
20,000	154.37	1,852.44	384.00	1,468.44
22,500	173.66	2,083.92	432.00	1,651.92
25,000	192.96	2,315.52	480.00	1,835.52
27,500	212.25	2,547.00	528.00	2,019.00
30,000	231.55	2,778.60	576.00	2,202.60
35,000	270.14	3,241.68	672.00	2,569.68
40,000	308.73	3,704.76	768.00	2,936.76
45,000	347.32	4,167.84	864.00	3,303.84
50,000	385.91	4,630.92	960.00	3,670.92
55,000	424.50	5,094.00	1,056.00	4,038.00
60,000	463.09	5,557.08	1,152.00	4,405.08

*Approximate

Mortgage Payment Table*
8½% - 20 Years

Mortgage Amount	Total Monthly Cost	Yearly Cost	Principal/Yr. (Averaged over 1st Ten Years)	Interest/Yr. (Averaged over 1st Ten Years)
$15,000	$130.18	$1,562.16	$ 450.00	$1,112.16
17,500	151.87	1,822.44	525.00	1,297.44
20,000	173.57	2,082.84	600.00	1,482.84
22,500	195.27	2,343.24	675.00	1,668.24
25,000	216.96	2,603.52	750.00	1,853.52
27,500	238.66	2,863.92	825.00	2,038.92
30,000	260.35	3,124.20	900.00	2,224.20
35,000	303.74	3,644.88	1,050.00	2,594.88
40,000	347.13	4,165.56	1,200.00	2,965.56
45,000	390.53	4,686.36	1,350.00	3,336.36
50,000	433.92	5,207.04	1,500.00	3,707.04
55,000	477.31	5,727.72	1,650.00	4,077.72
60,000	520.70	6,248.40	1,800.00	4,448.40

Mortgage Payment Table*
8½% - 25 Years

Mortgage Amount	Total Monthly Cost	Yearly Cost	Principal/Yr. (Averaged over 1st Ten Years)	Interest/Yr. (Averaged over 1st Ten Years)
$15,000	$120.79	$1,449.48	$ 273.00	$1,176.48
17,500	140.92	1,691.04	318.50	1,372.54
20,000	161.05	1,932.60	364.00	1,568.60
22,500	181.18	2,174.16	409.50	1,764.66
25,000	201.31	2,415.72	455.00	1,960.72
27,500	221.44	2,657.28	500.50	2,157.28
30,000	241.57	2,898.84	546.00	2,352.84
35,000	281.83	3,381.96	637.00	2,744.96
40,000	322.10	3,865.20	728.00	3,137.20
45,000	362.36	4,348.32	819.00	3,529.32
50,000	402.62	4,831.44	910.00	3,921.44
55,000	442.88	5,314.56	1,001.00	4,313.56
60,000	483.14	5,797.68	1,092.00	4,705.68

*Approximate